The Reef

Teacher's Guide

Unit 18

-ness	-less
•	•
as in fairness	Means without as in helpless

Note: See New and Important Objectives on page 2 for a complete list of skills taught and reviewed.

Critical Foundations in Primary Reading

Marilyn Sprick, Ann Watanabe, Karen Akiyama-Paik, and Shelley V. Jones

A Cambium Learning® Company

BOSTON, MA • LONGMONT, CO

ISBN 13-digit: 978-1-60218-541-8
ISBN 10-digit: 1-60218-541-7

7 8 9 10 11 B&B 16 15 14 13 12

167011/6-12

Table of Contents
Unit 18
The Reef

How to Teach the Lessons

End of the Unit

Letter Sounds and Combinations

Cumulative Review of *Read Well 1* Sounds and Combinations (Ss, Ee, ee, Mm, Aa, Dd, th, Nn, Tt, Ww, Ii, Th, Hh, Cc, Rr, ea, sh, Sh, Kk, -ck, oo, ar, wh, Wh, ĕ, -y as in fly, Ll, Oo, Bb, all, Gg, Ff, Uu, er, oo as in book, Yy, a schwa, Pp, ay, Vv, Qq, Jj, Xx, or, Zz, a_e, -y as in baby, i_e, ou, ow as in cow, ch, Ch, ai, igh, o_e, ir) and:

Unit 2	Unit 3			Unit 5	Unit 6
aw /aw/ **Paw** Voiced	ew /ōō/ **Crew** Voiced	ue /ōō/ **Blue** Voiced	u_e /ōō/ **Flute** Bossy E Voiced	ow /ōōō/ **Snow** Voiced (Long)	ge /j/ **Page** Voiced

Unit 6	Unit 7		Unit 8		Unit 10
-dge /j/ **Badge** Voiced	ci /sss/ **Circle** Unvoiced	ce /sss/ **Center** Unvoiced	kn /nnn/ **Knee** Voiced	ph /fff/ **Phone** Unvoiced	oa /ōōō/ **Boat** Voiced (Long)

Unit 11		Unit 12		Unit 13
oi /oi/ **Point** Voiced	ea /ĕĕĕ/ **Bread** Voiced (Short)	gi /j/ **Giraffe** Voiced	au /au/ **Astronaut** Voiced	oy /oy/ **Boy** Voiced

Affixes (including morphographs—affixes taught with meaning) and Open Syllables

Cumulative Review of *Read Well 1* Affixes (-ed, -en, -es, -ing, -ly, -s, -y, -tion) and:

Unit 2	Unit 3		Unit 5		Unit 6
re- **Means again** as in reread	un- **Means not** as in unhappy	ex- as in excited	o Open syllable /ō/ as in open and moment	-ful **Means full of** as in colorful	bi- **Means two** as in bicycle

Unit 7	Unit 8	Unit 11	Unit 12	Unit 13	
de- as in detective	-able as in comfortable	i Open syllable /i/ as in silence and pilot	be- as in before	-ous as in enormous	dis- as in discover

Unit 14		Unit 15		Unit 16	
-al as in animal	-ible as in flexible	-or **Means one who** as in actor	-ment as in apartment	-ic as in scientific	pre- **Means before** as in preview

Unit 17		Unit 18		Unit 19	
-ity as in activity	-sion as in permission	-ness as in fairness	-less **Means without** as in helpless	in- as in insert	im- **Means not** as in impossible

Introduction
The Reef

Story Notes

The Great Barrier Reef: This short expository piece introduces the setting for Unit 18—the Great Barrier Reef of Australia. Students learn about ecosystems and underwater habitats.

Miss Tam at the Great Barrier Reef: Everyone's favorite librarian, Miss Tam, heads Down Under for her next adventure.

Wonders of the Coral Reef: In this expository selection, students get more closely acquainted with reef dwellers such as the coral polyp and the sea slug.

Pete the Pufferfish: Students follow the amusing antics of Pete the Pufferfish, who tries out a number of defense mechanisms used by marine animals to protect themselves from predators. Pete eventually discovers his own unique method for fending off bigger fish.

Miss Tam Goes Home: This unit's fluency passage reviews the highlights of Miss Tam's great adventure in Australia.

Recommended Read Alouds

The *Read Well 2* suggested Read Alouds enhance Small Group instruction—providing opportunities to further build background knowledge and vocabulary.

CAUTION (Reminder)
Do not read the Read Aloud recommendations during small group instruction. Reserve this time for students to read.

Coral Reef Food Chains by Kelley MacAulay and Bobbie Kalman

Nonfiction • Expository

Food chains are the starting point for learning more about different animals and plants that live on a coral reef. From phytoplankton to the apex predators like the tiger shark, these colorful aquatic creatures will fascinate students.

Read Well Connections

Plentiful photographs and diagrams in the Read Aloud help convey the tremendous diversity of the reef ecosystem they read about in Unit 18. Students also reinforce the knowledge of food chains they gained in Unit 17.

NOTE FROM THE AUTHORS

DIFFERENTIATING PRACTICE

An important reminder: Within any group of students, there is a range of skills, even among the highest-performing groups.

The general rule of thumb is that the lowest-performing students in any group need more practice than the highest. Modeling from the other students will not even up the differences. Without a teacher's conscious attention to differentiating practice, the highest-performing students in the group will continue to get the most practice. The lowest-performing students in the group have the slowest response rates—they are always in the back seat.

To keep all students in your group feeling confident and competent, increase fluency practice for some but not for others. For more ideas, see "Important Tips" on page 11 of the Unit 16 Teacher's Guide.

New and Important Objectives

A Research-Based Reading Program

Phonemic Awareness
Phonics
Fluency
Vocabulary
Comprehension

Phonological and Phonemic Awareness

Blending; Rhyming; Onset and Rime; Counting Syllables

Phonics

Cumulative Letter Sounds and Combinations

Review • Ss, Ee, ee, Mm, Aa, Dd, th, Nn, Tt, Ww, Ii, Th, Hh, Cc, Rr, ea, sh, Sh, Kk, -ck, oo, ar, wh, Wh, ĕ, -y (as in fly), Ll, Oo, Bb, all, Gg, Ff, Uu, er, oo (as in book), Yy, a (schwa), Pp, ay, Vv, Qq, Jj, Xx, or, Zz, a_e, -y (as in baby), i_e, ou, ow (as in cow), ch, Ch, ai, igh, o_e, ir, aw, ew, ue, u_e, ow (as in snow), ge, -dge, ci, ce, kn, ph, oa, oi, ea (as in bread), gi, au, oy

Cumulative Affixes, Morphographs, and Open Syllables

Review • -ed, -en, -er, -es, -est, -ing, -ly, -s, -y, -tion, re-, un-, ex-, o (as in open), -ful, bi-, de-, -able, i (as in silence), be-, -ous, dis-, -al, -ible, -or, -ment, -ic, pre-, -ity, -sion

★New Letter Sounds, Combinations, Affixes, and Morphographs

-ness (as in fairness) • cleverness, emptiness, neatness, rudeness, wilderness

-less (as in helpless) • brainless, endless, harmless, helpless, needless, nonetheless

★New Proper Nouns

Aussie, Aussies, Australia, Great Barrier Reef, Paddy, Paddy's, Pete, Pete's, Sasha

★New Pattern Words

blend, blended, choices, crook, crooked, dice, dwarf, fan, fans, gear, growths, gulp, gulped ◆ ice, ouch, perch, plank, reef, reefs ◆ screwed, shine, shines, snatch, snatches ◆ soak ◆ spines, spit, squish, squished, stairs ◆ strap, swoops, tort, twirl, twirling ◆ vest, waist, wedged ◆ yay, zip, zipped

***Known Pattern Words With Affixes** • balled, blindly, bobbing, boots, bumped, changes, darted, eels, guessed, guided, hoses, hurts, puffed, rays, rereading, rubbing, shells, shopping, snoring, sorted, squirted, starry, sun's, swimming, swooshed, twisted

* **Known Pattern Words With Affixes**, **Known Tricky Words With Affixes**, and **Known Multisyllabic Words With Affixes** have base words students have previously read. The words are new in this unit because they have not been previously read with the affix.

★ = New in this unit

◆ = Words that are not introduced in the exercises before they are read in the storybook

Phonics *(continued)*

★New Compound and Hyphenated Words

◆ clownfish, grown-up, halfway, hooly-dooly, itself ◆ jellyfish, longnose hawkfish, parrotfish, pufferfish, seagrass, seahorse, seaweeds, shape-shifting, sheepskin, staghorn, upright, wetsuit, wetsuits

★Other New Multisyllabic Words

advisor, advisors, approximately, attached, builder, builders, confused, contort, contortion, contortionist, contortions, coral, disguise, diver, division ◆ flippers, frustrated ◆ fussy, inflatable, inflate, instructions, instructor, leafy ◆ lemon, lobster, manta, mollusks, moray, mumble, mumbled, normal, occasion, octopus, octopuses, omnivore, omnivores, penguin, phytoplankton, position, recipe, regulator, sausage, scuba, slender, slither, slithering, sophisticated, spiny, stingers, suckers, surrounded, swallow, swallows, tacos, taxi, tentacles, thirty ◆ turtle, vanilla, vision, wriggle, wriggled

***Known Multisyllabic Words With Affixes** • bellowed, children's, dazzling, explored, finishing, fluttering, giggling, heavily, imagining, motioned, openings, photos, reappeared, recalled, relaxed, rubbery

★New Tricky Words

algae, among, anemones, ecosystem, gradually, journal, leisurely, minke, nudibranch, nudibranchs, pears, polyp, polyps, pudding, sponge, sponges, suit, suiting

***Known Tricky Words With Affixes** • covering, discouraged, preview, wonders

Fluency

Accuracy, Expression, Phrasing, Rate

Vocabulary

New • Australia, advisor, algae, approximately, confused, contortion, coral polyp, coral reef, disguise, ecosystem, frustrated, inflatable, leisurely, nudibranch, omnivore, regulator, review

Review • adventure, advice, amazing, ancient, bittersweet, carnivore, colony, commotion, community, continent, dangerous, determined, eventful, exhausted, extinct, flexible, food chain, habitat, herbivore, integrity, link, planet, possible, predator, protect, ravenous, spunky, summon, surface

Reviewed in Context • adventure, advice, Africa, allow, amazed, amazing, ancient, bellow, bittersweet, caption, carnivore, colony, commotion, community, connect, continent, creature, dangerous, despite, determined, distressed, energy, eventful, except, exhausted, food chain, Ghana, glisten, habitat, herbivore, imagine, immigrate, integrity, luscious, planet, predator, prey, protect, protected, relative, reptile, shrug, splendid, spunky, summon, surface, survive, tattered, unique, wonderful, village

Idioms and Expressions Review • educated guess

Comprehension

Unit Genres

Nonfiction • Expository
Fiction • Realistic Narrative
Fiction • Narrative

Comprehension Processes

Build Knowledge: Factual, Procedural, Conceptual

Day	1	2	3	4	5	6
Remember						
Defining	S					
Identifying (recalling)	S,C	S,C	S,C	S	S,C	C
Using	S	S		S	S	
Understand						
Defining (in your own words)	S,C	S	S	S,C		
Describing	S	S,C	S,C	S,C	S	
Explaining (rephrasing)	S	S,C	S,C	S,C	S,C	C
Illustrating	C		C			
Sequencing		C	C	S	S	
Summarizing	S	S,C	S,C	S	S	C
Using	S,C	S	S	S,C	E,S,C	C
Visualizing			C			
Apply						
Demonstrating						
Explaining (unstated)	S,C	S		S	S	
Illustrating						
Inferring	S,C	S	S		S	C
Making Connections (relating)						
Predicting		S		S	S	
Using	S,C	S,C	S	S	S	
Analyze						
Classifying	S		S	S		
Comparing/Contrasting						
Distinguishing Cause/Effect						
Drawing Conclusions				S		
Inferring						
Evaluate						
Making Judgments				C	E	
Responding (personal)	S	S,C	S		C	
Create						
Generating Ideas	S	C	S		C	

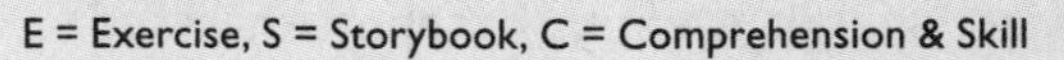

E = Exercise, S = Storybook, C = Comprehension & Skill

Comprehension *(continued)*

Skills and Strategies

Day	1	2	3	4	5	6
Priming Background Knowledge			S	S		
Setting a Purpose for Reading	S	S	S	S	S	
Answering Questions	S	S	S	S	S	
Asking Questions	S		S			
Visualizing			C			
Comprehension Monitoring/Fix Ups						
Does it Make Sense?	C	C		C		
Looking Back						
Restating						
Summarizing						
Main Idea						
Retelling						
Supporting Details	S		S			
Understanding Text Structure						
Title, Author, Illustrator	S	S	S	S	S	
Fact or Fiction						
Genre (Classifying)	S		S	S		
Narrative						
Setting		S,C	C	S,C	C	
Main Character/Traits (Characterization)		S,C	C	S	S,C	
Goal		S,C		S	S	
Problem/Solution						
Action/Events/Sequence		C	C		S	
Outcome/Conclusion			C			
Lesson/Author's Message						
Expository						
Subject/Topic						C
Heading						
Supporting Details (Facts/Information)	S,C	S	S			C
Main Idea						
Using Graphic Organizers						
Chart						
Diagram (labeling)	C	C				
Hierarchy (topic/detail)						C
K-W-L						
Map (locating, labeling)						
Matrix (compare/contrast)						
Sequence (linear, cycle, cause and effect)						
Story Map		C				
Web		C		C		

E = Exercise, S = Storybook, C = Comprehension & Skill

Comprehension *(continued)*

Study Skills

Day	1	2	3	4	5	6
Alphabetical Order						
Following Directions						
Locating Information	C			S,C		
Note Taking						
Previewing						
Reviewing		S	S	S	S	
Test Taking						C
Using Glossary	S	S	S	S		
Using Table of Contents	S	S	S	S		
Viewing	S,C	S	S	S	S	
Verifying						

Writing in Response to Reading

Day	1	2	3	4	5	6
Sentence Completion	C	C				C
Making Lists						
Sentence Writing	C	C	C	C	C	C
Story Retell/Summary			C			
Fact Summary						C
Paragraph Writing		C	C		C	C
Report Writing						
Open-Ended Response		C			C	
Creative Writing						

Writing Traits

(Addressed within the context of Writing in Response to Reading)

Day	1	2	3	4	5	6
Ideas and Content						
Elaborating/Generating		C	C		C	
Organization						
Introduction						
Topic Sentence						C
Supporting Details						C
Sequencing		C	C			
Word Choice						
Sophisticated Words (Tier 2 and 3)		C	C		C	C
Conventions						
Capital	C	C	C	C	C	C
Ending Punctuation	C	C	C	C	C	C
Other (commas, quotation marks)						
Presentation						
Handwriting		C	C		C	C
Neatness		C	C		C	C

E = Exercise, S = Storybook, C = Comprehension & Skill

Daily Lesson Planning

LESSON PLAN FORMAT

Teacher-Directed 45 Minutes		Independent Teacher-Directed, as needed
Lesson Part 1 (Phonological Awareness, Phonics, Fluency, Comprehension) 15–20 Minutes	**Lesson Part 2** (Vocabulary, Fluency, Comprehension) 20–25 Minutes	**Lesson Part 3** (Vocabulary, Fluency, Comprehension) 15–20 Minutes
• Exercises	• Unit and/or Story Opener • Vocabulary • Interactive Story Reading • Short Passage Practice Timed Readings	• Story Reading With Partner or Whisper Reading • Comprehension and Skill Activities

HOMEWORK

Read Well Homework (blackline masters of new *Read Well 2* passages) provides an opportunity for children to celebrate accomplishments with parents. Homework should be sent home on routine days.

ORAL READING FLUENCY ASSESSMENT

Upon completion of this unit, assess each student and proceed to Unit 19, as appropriate.

WRITTEN ASSESSMENT

During the time students would normally complete Comprehension and Skill Activities, students will be administered a written assessment that can be found on page 119 in the students' *Activity Book 3*.

Note: See Making Decisions for additional assessment information.

DIFFERENTIATED LESSON PLANS

The differentiated lesson plans illustrate how to use materials for students with various learning needs. As you set up your unit plan, always include *Read Well 2* Exercises and Story Reading on a daily basis. Unit 18 includes 6-, 8-, 9-, 10-, and 11-Day Plans.

Plans	For groups that:
6-DAY	Complete Oral Reading Fluency Assessments with Passes and Strong Passes
8-DAY	Complete Oral Reading Fluency Assessments with Passes and require teacher-guided assistance with Story Reading and Comprehension and Skill Work
9-, 10-, or 11-DAY	Have difficulty passing the unit Oral Reading Fluency Assessments

6-DAY PLAN		
Day 1 **Teacher-Directed** • Exercise 1 • Unit and Story Opener: The Reef; The Great Barrier Reef • Vocabulary, Ch. 1, 2 • The Great Barrier Reef, Ch. 1 • Guide practice, as needed, on Comp & Skill 1, 2 **Independent Work** • On Your Own: Partner or Whisper Read, The Great Barrier Reef, Ch. 2 • Comp & Skill 1, 2 **Homework** • Homework Passage 1	**Day 2** **Teacher-Directed** • Exercise 2 • Story Opener: Miss Tam at the Great Barrier Reef • Vocabulary, Ch. 1, 2 • Miss Tam at the Great Barrier Reef, Ch. 1 • Guide practice, as needed, on Comp & Skill 3, 4 **Independent Work** • On Your Own: Partner or Whisper Read, Miss Tam at the Great Barrier Reef, Ch. 2 • Comp & Skill 3, 4 **Homework** • Homework Passage 2	**Day 3** **Teacher-Directed** • Exercise 3 • Story Opener: Wonders of the Coral Reef • Vocabulary, Ch. 1, 2 • Wonders of the Coral Reef, Ch. 1 • Guide practice, as needed, on Comp & Skill 5a, 5b **Independent Work** • On Your Own: Partner or Whisper Read, Wonders of the Coral Reef, Ch. 2 • Comp & Skill 5a, 5b **Homework** • Homework Passage 3
Day 4 **Teacher-Directed** • Exercise 4 • Story Opener: Pete the Pufferfish • Vocabulary, Ch. 1, 2 • Pete the Pufferfish, Ch. 1 • Guide practice, as needed, on Comp & Skill 6, 7 **Independent Work** • On Your Own: Partner or Whisper Read, Pete the Pufferfish, Ch. 2 • Comp & Skill 6, 7 **Homework** • Homework Passage 4	**Day 5** **Teacher-Directed** • Exercise 5a • Exercise 5b: Focus Lesson • Vocabulary, Ch. 3, 4 • Pete the Pufferfish, Ch. 3 • Guide practice, as needed, on Comp & Skill 8, 9 **Independent Work** • On Your Own: Partner or Whisper Read, Pete the Pufferfish, Ch. 4 • Comp & Skill 8, 9 **Homework** • Homework Passage 5	**Day 6** **Teacher-Directed** • Exercise 6 • Fluency, Miss Tam Goes Home **Independent Work** • Repeated Reading: Partner or Whisper Read, Miss Tam Goes Home • Written Assessment • Oral Reading Fluency Assessment* **Homework** • Homework Passage 6

Note: Unit 18 features two Just for Fun Comp & Skill activities, one after Activity 5b and one after Activity 9. The first activity may be used anytime after "Wonders of the Coral Reef," Chapter 2, and the second may be used anytime after "Pete the Pufferfish," Chapter 4.

* The Oral Reading Fluency Assessments are individually administered by the teacher while students are working on their Written Assessments.

8-DAY PLAN • *Pre-Intervention*

Day 1	Day 2	Day 3	Day 4
Teacher-Directed • Exercise 1 • Unit and Story Opener: The Reef; The Great Barrier Reef • Vocabulary, Ch. 1, 2 • The Great Barrier Reef, Ch. 1 • Guide practice, as needed, on Comp & Skill 1 **Independent Work** • Repeated Reading: Partner or Whisper Read, The Great Barrier Reef, Ch. 1 • Comp & Skill 1 **Homework** • Homework Passage 1	**Teacher-Directed** • Review Exercise 1 • Review Vocabulary, Ch. 1, 2 • The Great Barrier Reef, Ch. 2 • Guide practice, as needed, on Comp & Skill 2 **Independent Work** • Repeated Reading: Partner or Whisper Read, The Great Barrier Reef, Ch. 2 • Comp & Skill 2 **Homework** • Extra Practice Word Fluency A	**Teacher-Directed** • Exercise 2 • Story Opener: Miss Tam at the Great Barrier Reef • Vocabulary, Ch. 1, 2 • Miss Tam at the Great Barrier Reef, Ch. 1 • Guide practice, as needed, on Comp & Skill 3, 4 **Independent Work** • On Your Own: Partner or Whisper Read, Miss Tam at the Great Barrier Reef, Ch. 2 • Comp & Skill 3, 4 **Homework** • Homework Passage 2	**Teacher-Directed** • Exercise 3 • Story Opener: Wonders of the Coral Reef • Vocabulary, Ch. 1, 2 • Wonders of the Coral Reef, Ch. 1 • Guide practice, as needed, on Comp & Skill 5a, 5b **Independent Work** • On Your Own: Partner or Whisper Read, Wonders of the Coral Reef, Ch. 2 • Comp & Skill 5a, 5b **Homework** • Homework Passage 3
Day 5	**Day 6**	**Day 7**	**Day 8**
Teacher-Directed • Exercise 4 • Story Opener: Pete the Pufferfish • Vocabulary, Ch. 1, 2 • Pete the Pufferfish, Ch. 1 • Guide practice, as needed, on Comp & Skill 6, 7 **Independent Work** • On Your Own: Partner or Whisper Read, Pete the Pufferfish, Ch. 2 • Comp & Skill 6, 7 **Homework** • Homework Passage 4	**Teacher-Directed** • Exercise 5a • Exercise 5b: Focus Lesson • Vocabulary, Ch. 3, 4 • Pete the Pufferfish, Ch. 3 • Guide practice, as needed, on Comp & Skill 8 **Independent Work** • Repeated Reading: Partner or Whisper Read, Pete the Pufferfish, Ch. 3 • Comp & Skill 8 **Homework** • Homework Passage 5	**Teacher-Directed** • Review Exercise 5a • Review Vocabulary, Ch. 3, 4 • Reread Pete the Pufferfish, Ch. 4 • Guide practice, as needed, on Comp & Skill 9 **Independent Work** • Repeated Reading: Partner or Whisper Read, Pete the Pufferfish, Ch. 4 • Comp & Skill 9 **Homework** • Extra Practice Word Fluency B	**Teacher-Directed** • Exercise 6 • Fluency, Miss Tam Goes Home **Independent Work** • Repeated Reading: Partner or Whisper Read, Miss Tam Goes Home • Written Assessment • Oral Reading Fluency Assessment* **Homework** • Homework Passage 6

9-, 10-, or 11-DAY PLAN • *Intervention*

For Days 1–8, follow 8-Day plan. Add Days 9, 10, 11 as follows:

Day 9 Extra Practice 1	Day 10 Extra Practice 2	Day 11 Extra Practice 3
Teacher-Directed • Decoding Practice • Fluency Passage **Independent Work** • Activity and Word Fluency A **Homework** • Fluency Passage	**Teacher-Directed** • Decoding Practice • Fluency Passage **Independent Work** • Activity and Word Fluency B **Homework** • Fluency Passage	**Teacher-Directed** • Decoding Practice • Fluency Passage **Independent Work** • Activity and Word Fluency A or B • Oral Reading Fluency Assessment* **Homework** • Fluency Passage

Materials and Materials Preparation

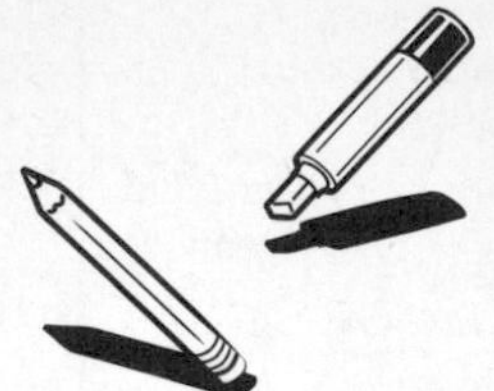

Core Lessons

Teacher Materials

READ WELL 2 **MATERIALS**

- Unit 18 Teacher's Guide
- Sound Cards
- Unit 18 Oral Reading Fluency Assessment found on page 127
- Group Assessment Record found in the *Assessment Manual*

SCHOOL SUPPLIES

Stopwatch or watch with a second hand

Student Materials

READ WELL 2 **MATERIALS (for each student)**

- *The Reef* storybook
- *Exercise Book 3*
- *Activity Book 3* or copies of Unit 18 Comp and Skill Work
- Unit 18 Written Assessment found in *Activity Book 3*, page 119, and on the blackline master CD
- Unit 18 Certificate of Achievement (BLM, page 128)
- Unit 18 Goal Setting (BLM, page 129)
- Unit 18 Homework (blackline masters)
  See *Getting Started* for suggested homework routines.

SCHOOL SUPPLIES

Pencils, colors (optional—markers, crayons, or colored pencils)

Make one copy per student of each blackline master, as appropriate for the group.

Note: For new or difficult Comprehension and Skill Activities, make overhead transparencies from the blackline masters. Use the transparencies to demonstrate and guide practice.

FOCUS LESSON

For Exercise 5b (Focus Lesson), make overhead transparencies from the blackline masters, write on transparencies placed over the pages, or use paper copies to demonstrate how to complete the lessons.

Extra Practice Lessons

CAUTION

Use these lessons only if needed. Students who need Extra Practice may benefit from one, two, or three lessons.

Student Materials

READ WELL 2 **MATERIALS (for each student, as needed)**

See Extra Practice blackline masters located on the CD.

- Unit 18 Extra Practice 1: Decoding Practice, Fluency Passage, Word Fluency A, and Activity
- Unit 18 Extra Practice 2: Decoding Practice, Fluency Passage, Word Fluency B, and Activity
- Unit 18 Extra Practice 3: Decoding Practice, Fluency Passage, Word Fluency A or B, and Activity

SCHOOL SUPPLIES

Pencils, colors (optional—markers, crayons, or colored pencils), highlighters

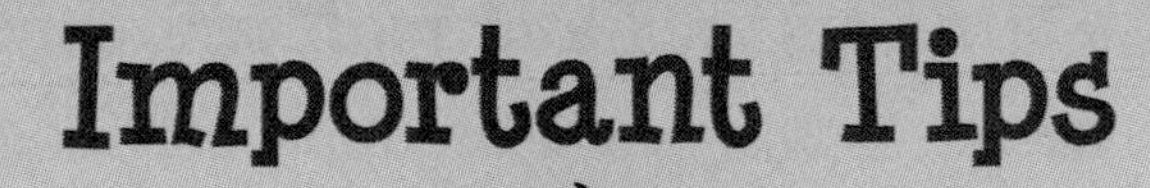

Active Engagement With Partner Think and Talk

Learning is enhanced when students are attentive and actively engaged. *Read Well* lessons are designed to support high rates of active engagement.

During *Read Well* lessons, students will be actively engaged by saying, doing, and writing things.

KEEP STUDENTS ACTIVELY ENGAGED BY HAVING . . .

STUDENTS SAY THINGS

Use choral, partner, and individual responses.

STUDENTS DO THINGS

Ask students to *do* things (e.g. thumbs up, touch and point, act) in response to questions.

STUDENTS WRITE THINGS

Read Well lessons include appropriate written activities. Students hear, see, say, and read during teacher-directed lessons. Then students write and illustrate during their independent work—practicing new skills and/or reviewing and extending abilities with previously taught skills.

This next section focuses on Partner Think and Talk—one strategy that will keep your students actively engaged.

Active engagement increases student achievement.

Partner Think and Talk:
Keeps your students engaged and monitors comprehension!

With Partner Think and Talk, *all* students think and talk about what they've read.

PARTNER THINK AND TALK PROCEDURES

1. Assign students partners.
2. Assign each partner a number, Partner 1 or Partner 2.
   (If you have an uneven number of students, one set of students will have two Partner 2's.)
3. Have students choral read a question.
   We're going to Think and Talk with our partners about what we just read.
   Touch question 1. Everyone, read the question and think about the answer.
4. Assign one partner to start.
   Now, discuss the answer with your partner. Partner 1, it's your turn first.
5. After an appropriate amount of time based on the complexity of the response, have the other partner share. Partner 2, now it's your turn to . . . [restate the question].
6. Call on a student to respond. [Stacia], how did you and your partner answer the question?

END-OF-CHAPTER THINK AND TALK QUESTIONS

Think and Talk questions prompt active thinking about text. These questions review central story elements and important facts, require inferential thinking, encourage students to ask questions, and encourage students to respond to what they've read.

Think and Talk Example

Say something like:

Everyone, read question 1 and think about the answer.
(What is the Great Barrier Reef?)

Partner 1, turn to Partner 2. Tell your partner what you remember about the Great Barrier Reef.

Wait for students to think and talk. Partner 2, turn to Partner 1. Can you add anything else to describe what the Great Barrier Reef is?

Wait for students to think and talk. [Courtney], how did you and your partner describe the Great Barrier Reef?
(We said that the Great Barrier Reef is made up of islands and coral reefs.)
[Ty], what did you and your partner come up with?
(We said that the Great Barrier Reef is alive.)
You know that the Great Barrier Reef is made up of islands and coral reefs, and you know that it is alive. Did anyone come up with other facts that would explain what the coral reef is? (We said that it was the home of thousands and thousands of animals.)

Great. You know that the Great Barrier Reef is a place made up of islands and coral reefs. It's made up of living things, and it is a home to thousands of different types of animals.

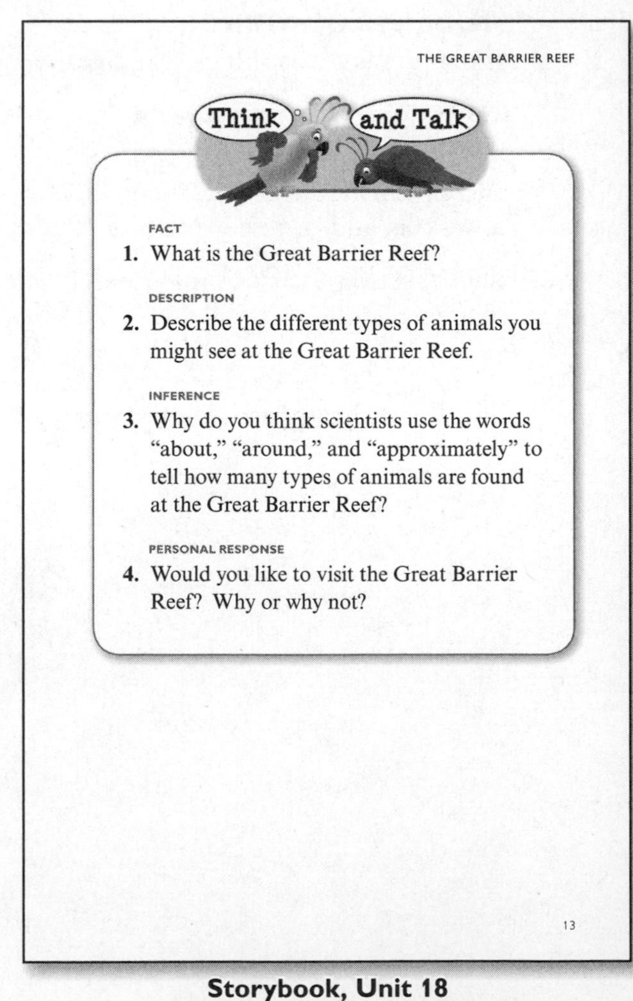
THE GREAT BARRIER REEF

FACT
1. What is the Great Barrier Reef?

DESCRIPTION
2. Describe the different types of animals you might see at the Great Barrier Reef.

INFERENCE
3. Why do you think scientists use the words "about," "around," and "approximately" to tell how many types of animals are found at the Great Barrier Reef?

PERSONAL RESPONSE
4. Would you like to visit the Great Barrier Reef? Why or why not?

13

Storybook, Unit 18
The Great Barrier Reef

How to Teach the Lessons

Teach from this section. Each instructional component is outlined in an easy-to-teach format.

Exercise 1

- Unit and Story Opener: The Reef, The Great Barrier Reef
- Vocabulary
- Story Reading 1
  With the Teacher: Chapter 1
  On Your Own: Chapter 2
- Comprehension and Skill Activities 1, 2

Exercise 2

- Story Opener: Miss Tam at the Great Barrier Reef
- Vocabulary
- Story Reading 2
  With the Teacher: Chapter 1
  On Your Own: Chapter 2
- Comprehension and Skill Activities 3, 4

Exercise 3

- Story Opener: Wonders of the Coral Reef
- Vocabulary
- Story Reading 3
  With the Teacher: Chapter 1
  On Your Own: Chapter 2
- Comprehension and Skill Activities 5a, 5b

Exercise 4

- Story Opener: Pete the Pufferfish
- Vocabulary
- Story Reading 4
  With the Teacher: Chapter 1
  On Your Own: Chapter 2
- Comprehension and Skill Activities 6, 7

Exercise 5a

- Exercise 5b: Focus Lesson
- Vocabulary
- Story Reading 5
  With the Teacher: Chapters 3, 4
- Comprehension and Skill Activities 8, 9

Exercise 6

- Story Reading 6
  With the Teacher: Miss Tam Goes Home (Fluency)
- Written Assessment

Note: Lessons include daily homework.

❶ **SOUND REVIEW** Use selected Sound Cards from Units 1–17.

PACING
Exercise 1 should take about 15 minutes.

❷ **SHIFTY WORD BLENDING**
For each word, have students say the underlined sound. Then have them sound out the word smoothly and say it. Use the words in sentences, as appropriate.

❸ **ACCURACY AND FLUENCY BUILDING**

C1. Reading by Analogy
Have students figure out how to read "phyto" by reading other words they know.

C2. Buildups
Tell students they can figure out bigger words by building from smaller words.
Have students read the words. Assist, as needed.
Read the underlined part, then the word. (ank, plank; plank, plankton; plankton, phytoplankton)
Wow, you read that hard word *phytoplankton. Phytoplankton* are tiny little plants that drift in the ocean. You can see them only through a microscope. Say the word two times. (phytoplankton, phytoplankton)

BUILD ACCURACY AND FLUENCY (Reminder)
For all rows and columns, follow the specific directions, then build accuracy and fluency with whole words.

E1. Tricky Words

- For each Tricky Word, have students use the sounds and word parts they know to silently sound out the word. Use the word in a sentence to help with pronunciation.
- If the word is unfamiliar, tell students the word.

ecosystem
Say the word parts silently. Thumbs up when you know the word. Use my sentence to help you pronounce the word. A group of animals and plants that live in the same area are called an . . . *ecosystem.* Read the word three times. (ecosystem, ecosystem, ecosystem)

polyps
Say the word parts silently. Thumbs up when you know the word. Use my sentence to help you pronounce the word. Coral reefs are formed by millions of coral . . . *polyps.* Read the word three times. (polyps, polyps, polyps)

covering We have to rake up all the leaves that are . . . *covering . . .* the lawn.
islands Have you ever been to the Hawaiian . . . *islands?*
ocean We walked along the beach and looked at the . . . *ocean.*

- Have students go back and read the whole words in the column.

❹ **MULTISYLLABIC WORDS**
For each word in Rows A and B, have students read the syllables, then the whole word. Use the word in a sentence, as appropriate. For Row C, have students read the whole words.

surface Micah sanded the wood until it had a smooth . . . *surface.*
mollusks Clams and snails are . . . *mollusks.*
approximately When people don't know the exact amount, they say . . . *approximately.*
Pacific The western coast of the United States is bordered by the . . . *Pacific . . .* Ocean.

❺ **WORDS IN CONTEXT**
For each word, have students use the sounds and word parts they know to silently sound out the word. Then have students read the sentence. Assist, as needed.

6 NAMES AND PLACES

7 GENERALIZATION: READING NEW WORDS IN PARAGRAPHS

- Have students read the paragraph silently, then out loud. Tell students to use the sounds and word parts they know to read any difficult words.
- Repeat practice, as needed.

The Great Barrier Reef

Unit 18 Exercise 1

Use before Chapters 1 and 2

1. SOUND REVIEW Use selected Sound Cards from Units 1–17.

2. SHIFTY WORD BLENDING For each word, have students say the underlined part, sound out smoothly, then read the word.

swoop	swoosh	swish	swim	swam

3. ACCURACY/FLUENCY BUILDING For each column, have students say any underlined part, then read each word. Next, have them read the column.

A1 Mixed Practice	B1 Compound Words	C1 Reading by Analogy	D1 Word Endings	E1 Tricky Words
alive	hawkfish	why	shines	ecosystem
jaws	longnose	phy	slugs	polyps
perch	seagrass	phyto	types	covering
rays	**B2 Morphographs & Affixes**	**C2 Buildups**	shells	islands
gulp	depend	plank	swallows	ocean
photo	harmless	plankton	snatches	
shrimp	delicious	phytoplankton	taste	
clams			tasty	

4. MULTISYLLABIC WORDS Have students read each word part, then read each whole word. For Row C, have students read each whole word.

A	sur•face	surface	mol•lusks	mollusks
B	ap•prox•i•mate•ly	approximately	Pa•cif•ic	Pacific
C	community	continent	habitat	imagine

5. WORDS IN CONTEXT For each word, have students use the sounds and word parts they know to figure out the word. Then have them read the sentence.

A	her•bi•vores	Animals that eat only plants are called herbivores.
B	car•ni•vores	Animals that eat mostly meat are called carnivores.
C	om•ni•vores	Animals that eat both plants and meat are called omnivores.

6. NAMES AND PLACES Have students use the sounds and word parts they know to figure out the words.

dwarf minke (mink-uh) whale	staghorn coral	Australia

7. GENERALIZATION Have students read the paragraph silently, then out loud. (New words: Great Barrier Reef, starry pufferfish)

I am working on a report about an animal that lives on the Great Barrier Reef. My report is about an incredible fish called the starry pufferfish. It eats coral and other small animals. It's awesome because it can puff up!

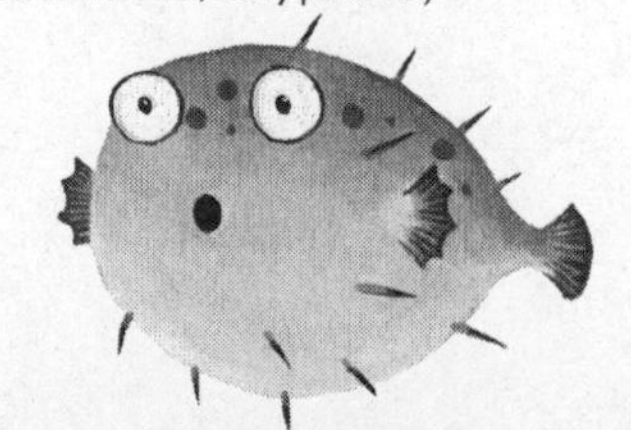

TEAM EXPECTATIONS
Acknowledge Team Efforts (Reminder)

Pair your compliments with team expectations. Say something like:
[Rowan], I like the way you followed directions.
[Diana], you are sitting up so I can hear your great reading.

GENERALIZATION (Reminder)

The generalization task provides an opportunity for you to informally assess students' ability to read new words that have not been pretaught.

COMPREHENSION PROCESSES

Remember, Understand, Apply, Create

PROCEDURES

1. Introducing the Storybook and Unit

Viewing; Identifying—Title, What; Defining and Using Vocabulary—habitat

Discuss the storybook and theme. Say something like:

What's the title of your storybook? (The Reef)

Look at the cover. What do you see? (the ocean, fish, coral . . .)

In this unit, we're going to read about an incredible *habitat*, the Great Barrier Reef.

Who remembers what a *habitat* is?

(It's a place where a plant or animal lives.)

That's right. The Great Barrier Reef is the habitat of thousands of different plants and animals.

2. Introducing the Story

Using Table of Contents; Identifying—Titles; Identifying—Genre; Inferring

Have students find the Table of Contents for Unit 18.

Say something like:

Look at the Table of Contents.

There are five stories in this unit.

Let's find the nonfiction stories in this unit.

What's the first nonfiction story called? (The Great Barrier Reef)

What's the next nonfiction story? (Wonders of the Coral Reef)

Read the red story titles to yourself.

There are also three fictional stories. The first one is "Miss Tam at the Great Barrier Reef." What do you think Miss Tam is going to do at the Great Barrier Reef?

(go swimming, hunt for shells . . .)

Let's get started with "The Great Barrier Reef." What page is it on?

(page 5)

Table of Contents

UNIT 18 • The Reef

2

3. Introducing the Title Page
Discuss the title page and the gray text questions.

The Great Barrier Reef

by Ann Watanabe

Look at the picture. It shows a bird's-eye view of the Great Barrier Reef. What is a bird's-eye view?[1] What do you see?[2] Across thousands of years, the Great Barrier Reef has been built by tiny animals. What questions do you have about the Great Barrier Reef?[3]

5

❶ **Understand:** Viewing: Defining and Using Idioms and Expressions—bird's-eye view (A bird's-eye view is looking at something from above, like a bird does.)

❷ **Understand:** Describing (I see an ocean, lots of water, islands . . .)

❸ **Create:** Generating Ideas, Asking Questions (What animals built the reef? How did they build it . . .)

COMPREHENSION PROCESSES

Understand, Apply

PROCEDURES

1. Introducing Vocabulary

★Australia ★coral reef
★ecosystem
★approximately, continent

- For each vocabulary word, have students read the word by parts, then read the whole word.
- Read the student-friendly explanations to students as they follow with their fingers. Then have students use the vocabulary word by following the gray text.
- Review and discuss the photos and illustrations.

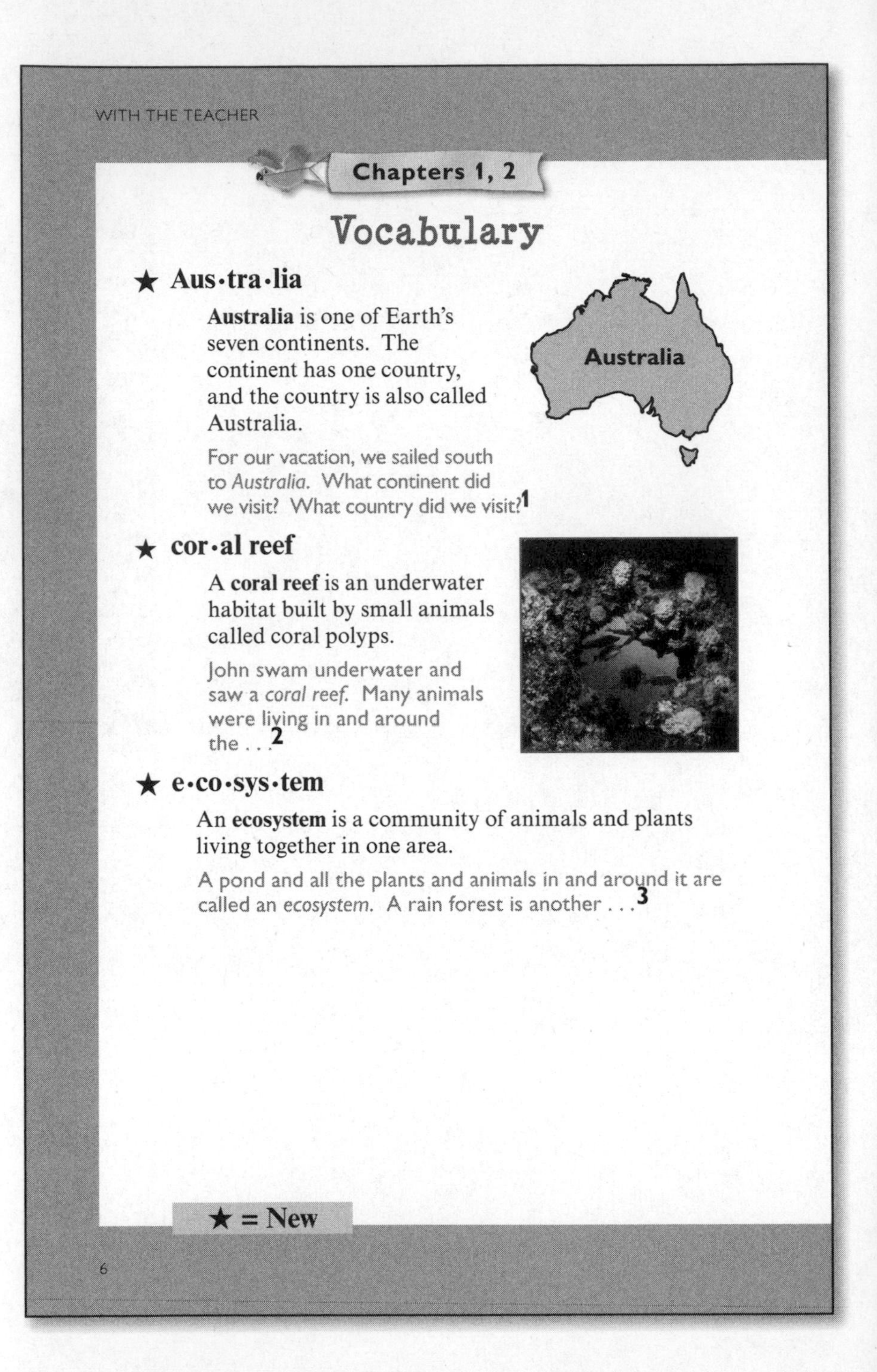

WITH THE TEACHER

Chapters 1, 2

Vocabulary

★ **Aus•tra•lia**

Australia is one of Earth's seven continents. The continent has one country, and the country is also called Australia.

For our vacation, we sailed south to *Australia.* What continent did we visit? What country did we visit?[1]

★ **cor•al reef**

A **coral reef** is an underwater habitat built by small animals called coral polyps.

John swam underwater and saw a *coral reef.* Many animals were living in and around the . . .[2]

★ **e•co•sys•tem**

An **ecosystem** is a community of animals and plants living together in one area.

A pond and all the plants and animals in and around it are called an *ecosystem.* A rain forest is another . . .[3]

★ = New

6

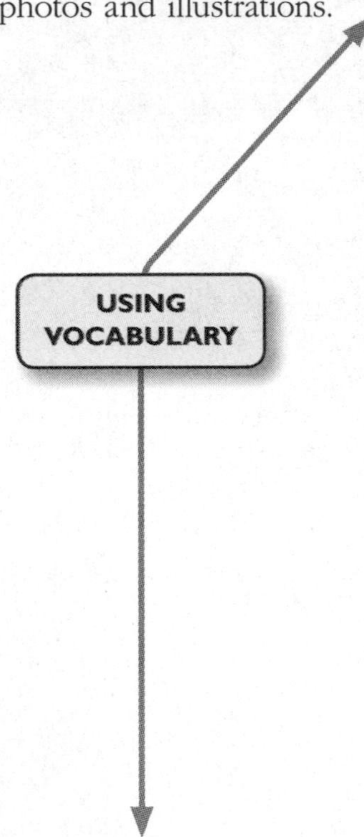

❶ **Understand:** Using Vocabulary—Australia (We visited the continent of Australia. We visited the country of Australia.)

❷ **Understand:** Using Vocabulary—coral reef (coral reef)

❸ **Apply:** Using Vocabulary—ecosystem (ecosystem)

★= New in this unit

2. Now You Try It!

- Read or paraphrase the directions.
- Have students read the word by parts, then read the whole word.
- Have students explain or define the word in their own words. Say something like:

  Look at the word. Say the parts, then read the whole word.
  (con•ti•nent, continent)
  Now let's pretend that we're going to explain or define the word *continent* to a friend. [Dave], what would you say?
  Start with "A *continent* is . . . " (A continent is an enormous piece of land.)
  That's right. A continent is an enormous area of land. It is one of seven large land areas on Earth.

- Have students turn to the appropriate page in the glossary and discuss how their definition is the same as or different from the glossary's. Your students may like their definition better.

Note: By defining a word in their own words, students are demonstrating depth of word knowledge. Verbatim responses only demonstrate memorization. Encourage paraphrasing.

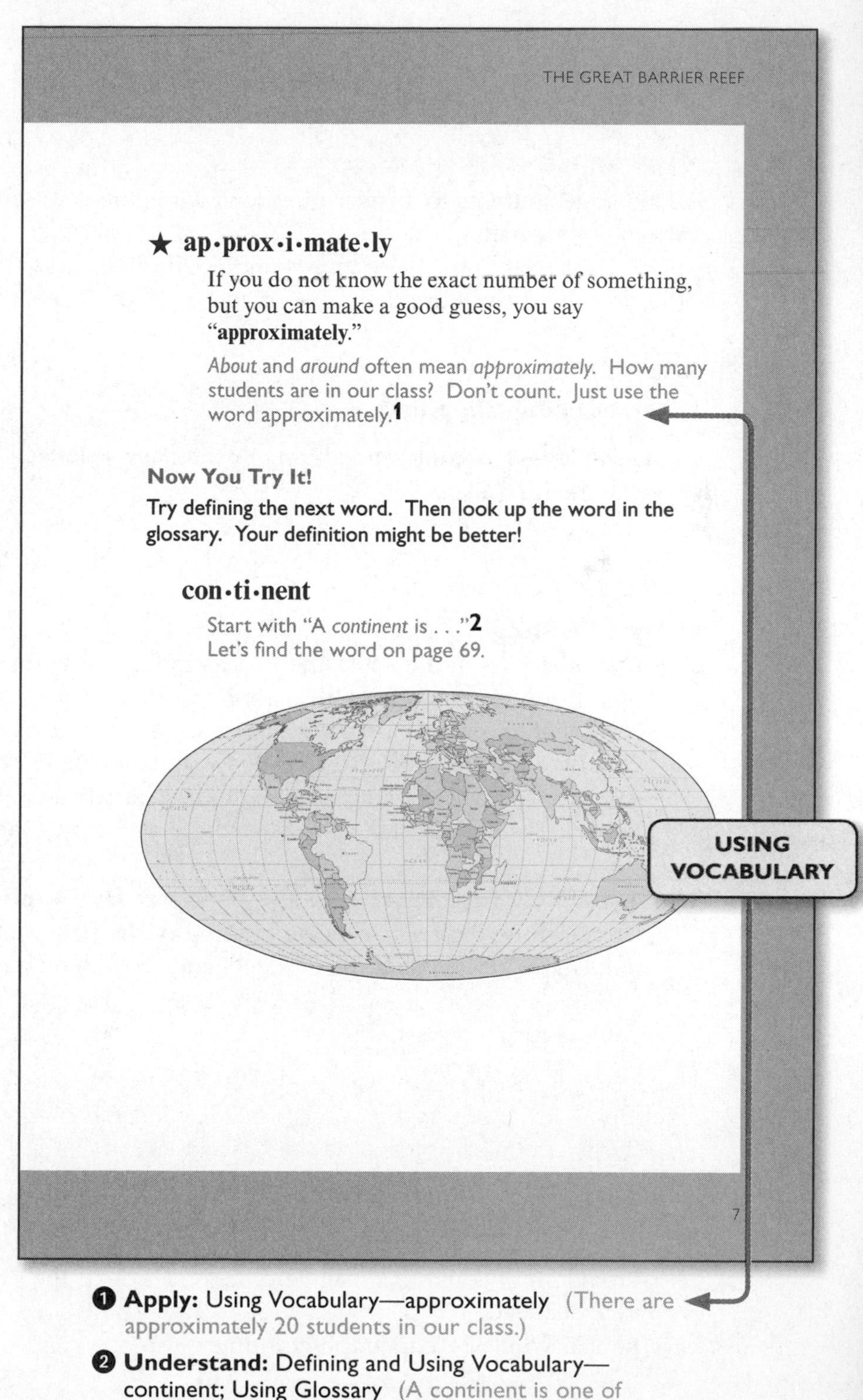

❶ **Apply:** Using Vocabulary—approximately (There are approximately 20 students in our class.)

❷ **Understand:** Defining and Using Vocabulary—continent; Using Glossary (A continent is one of seven large land areas on Earth.)

CHAPTER 1 INSTRUCTIONS

Students read Chapter 1 with the teacher and Chapter 2 on their own.
Note: If you're working on an 8- to 11-Day Plan, you will read Chapter 2 with students.

COMPREHENSION PROCESSES

Understand, Apply, Evaluate

COMPREHENSION BUILDING

- Encourage students to answer questions with complete sentences, when appropriate.
- If students have difficulty comprehending, think aloud with them or reread the portion of the story that answers the question. Repeat the question.

PROCEDURES

1. Introducing Chapter 1

Identifying—Title; Inferring; Using Vocabulary—planet

Say something like:
Turn to page 8. What's the title of this chapter? (The Blue Planet)
What do you think the blue planet is? (The blue planet is Earth.)

2. First Reading

- Ask questions and discuss the text as indicated by the gray text.
- Mix group and individual turns, independent of your voice.
  Have students work toward a group accuracy goal of 0–2 errors.
  Quietly keep track of errors made by all students in the group.
- After reading the story, practice any difficult words.
  Repeat, if students have not reached the accuracy goal.

CORRECTING DECODING ERRORS

During story reading, gently correct any error, then have students reread the sentence.

3. Second Reading, Short Passage Practice: Developing Prosody

- Demonstrate expressive, fluent reading of the first paragraph. Read at a rate slightly faster than the students' rate. Say something like:
  Listen to my expression as I read the first paragraph. I'm going to read like I'm narrating a special TV program or video about Earth.

  "Close your eyes and imagine yourself in space. Now open your eyes and look down on Earth—the blue planet. Earth looks blue from space because there is so much water covering its surface."
- Guide practice with your voice.
  Read the first page with me.
- Provide individual turns while others track with their fingers and whisper read.
- Repeat with one paragraph at a time.

REPEATED READINGS

Prosody

On the second reading, students practice developing prosody—phrasing and expression. Research has shown that prosody is related to both fluency and comprehension.

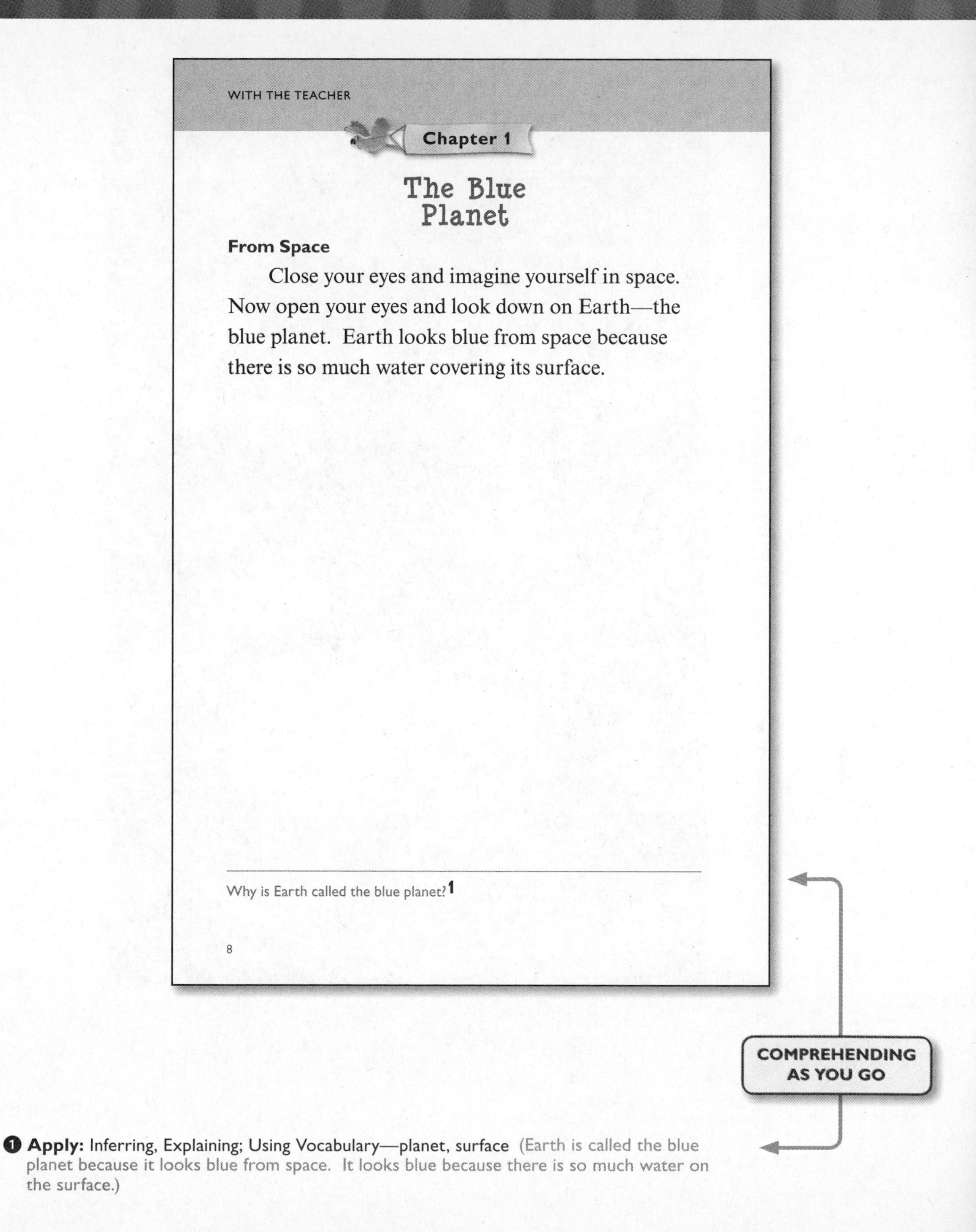
WITH THE TEACHER

Chapter 1

The Blue Planet

From Space

Close your eyes and imagine yourself in space. Now open your eyes and look down on Earth—the blue planet. Earth looks blue from space because there is so much water covering its surface.

Why is Earth called the blue planet? 1

8

COMPREHENDING AS YOU GO

❶ **Apply:** Inferring, Explaining; Using Vocabulary—planet, surface (Earth is called the blue planet because it looks blue from space. It looks blue because there is so much water on the surface.)

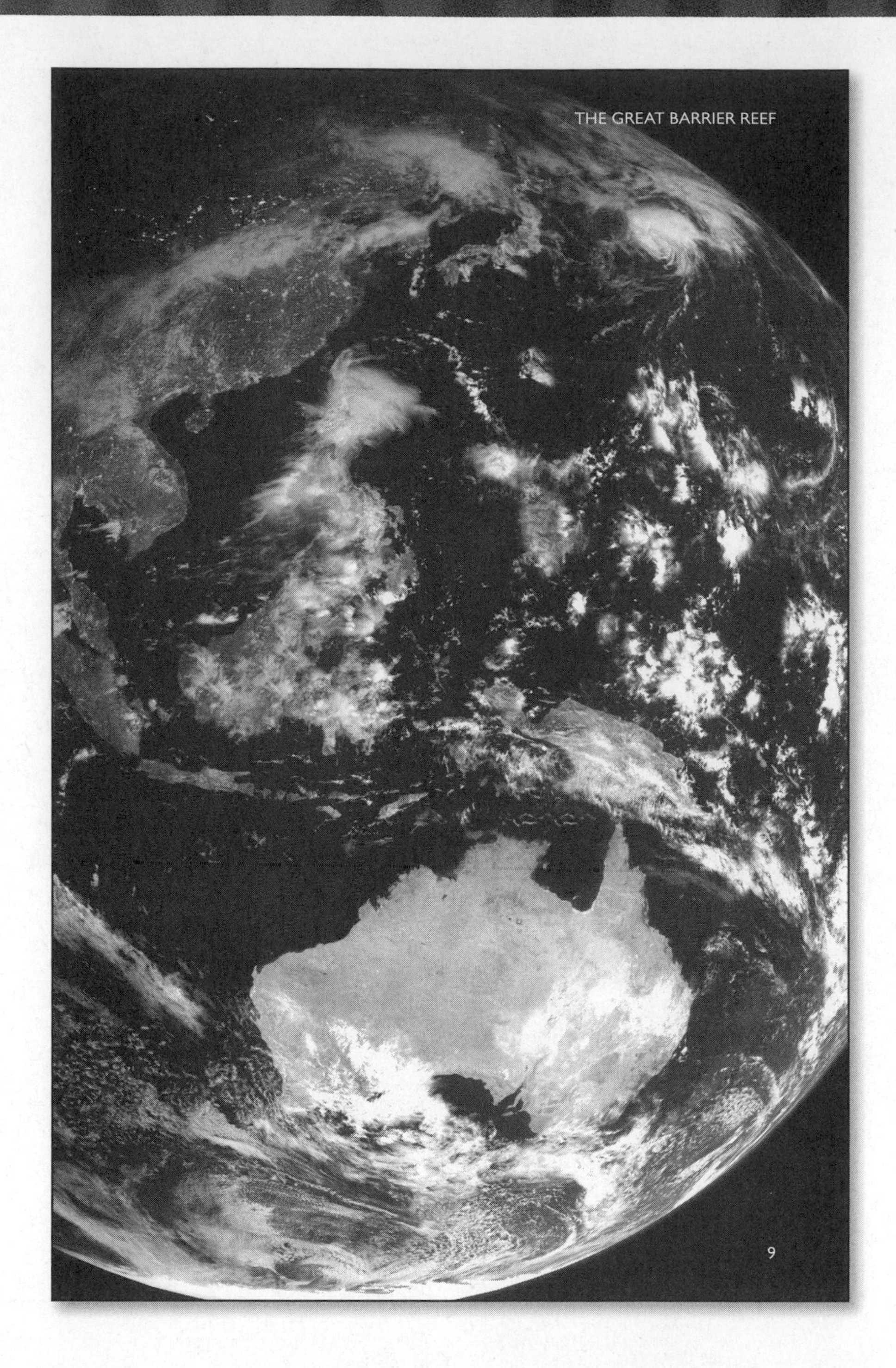
THE GREAT BARRIER REEF
9

WITH THE TEACHER

Look for the Pacific Ocean in the photo. Now find the continent of Australia.

Find the Great Barrier Reef of Australia. The Great Barrier Reef is made up of thousands of coral reefs and hundreds of islands. It is so large that you can see it from space. Unlike a continent, the coral reefs are alive.

Touch the Great Barrier Reef. Describe what it's made up of.[1]

10

COMPREHENDING AS YOU GO

❶ **Understand:** Describing; Using Vocabulary—coral reef (The Great Barrier Reef is made up of thousands of coral reefs and hundreds of islands.)

Rich With Life

The Great Barrier Reef stretches across 1,240 miles. Except for the rain forests, coral reefs have more types of animals than any other ecosystem. The Great Barrier Reef is home to:

About 1,500 types of fish

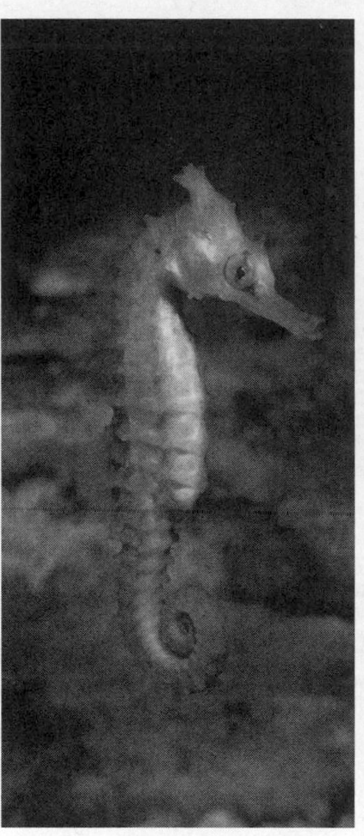

Seahorses

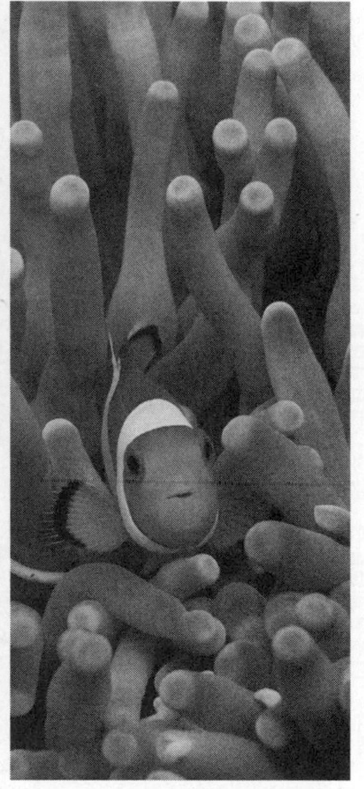

Clownfish

FOCUS ON WORD CHOICE

Using Vocabulary—approximately

After completing the page, say something like:
How many types of fish are found on the Great Barrier Reef? (About 1,500)
Scientist aren't sure of the exact number, so they use the word *about*. What's a snazzier way to say "about 1,500 types of fish"? (approximately 1,500 types of fish)

WITH THE TEACHER

Around 5,000 types of mollusks

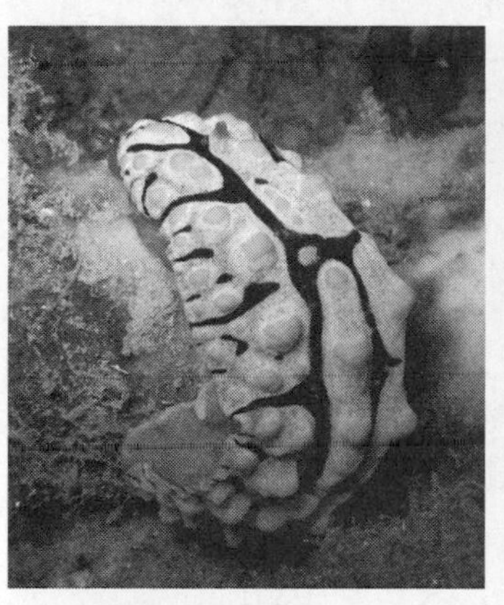

Sea slugs

Giant clams

Approximately 360 types of hard coral

Staghorn coral

Plate coral

Describe the different types of animals you might see at the Great Barrier Reef.**1**

12

FOCUS ON WORD CHOICE

Using Vocabulary—approximately

After completing the page, say something like:
How many types of mollusks are found on the Great Barrier Reef? (around 5,000)
Scientist aren't sure of the exact number, so another word they use is *around.* What's a snazzier way to say "around 5,000 types of mollusks"? (approximately 5,000 types of mollusks)

FOCUS ON INFERENCE

Classifying

Let's see if we can figure out what a mollusk is. Look at the sea slug. What kind of body do slugs have? (soft)
Now look at the clam. What kind of body do you think the clam has inside its hard shell? (It has a soft body.)
That's right. Mollusks are animals with soft bodies and no backbones.

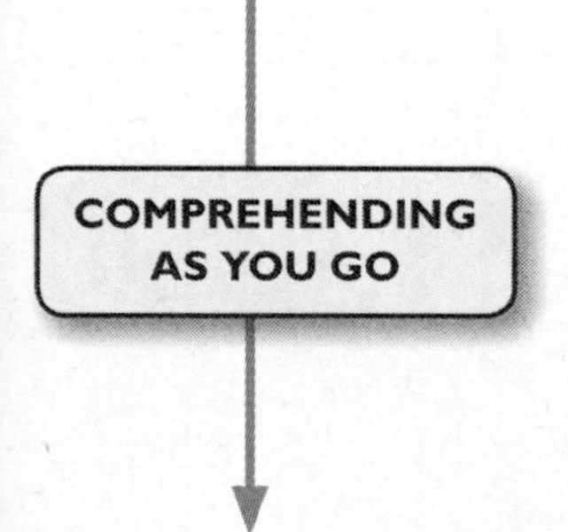

1 **Understand:** Describing, Summarizing (You might see a sea horse, which is a funny little fish with a long nose and a curly tail. You might see colorful clownfish, sea slugs, and giant clams. There's all kinds of beautiful, colorful coral . . .)

FACT

1. What is the Great Barrier Reef?

DESCRIPTION

2. Describe the different types of animals you might see at the Great Barrier Reef.

INFERENCE

3. Why do you think scientists use the words "about," "around," and "approximately" to tell how many types of animals are found at the Great Barrier Reef?

PERSONAL RESPONSE

4. Would you like to visit the Great Barrier Reef? Why or why not?

❶ **Understand:** Explaining—Fact (The Great Barrier Reef is made up of thousands of islands and coral reefs.)

❷ **Understand:** Describing, Summarizing (You might see a sea horse, which is a funny little fish with a long nose and a curly tail. There's colorful clownfish, sea slugs and giant clams. And there's all kinds of beautiful, colorful coral.)

❸ **Apply:** Inferring; **Understand:** Using Vocabulary—possible; Using Idioms and Expressions—educated guess (There are so many different kinds of animals at the Great Barrier Reef that it isn't possible to count them. Scientists have to make an educated guess.)

❹ **Evaluate:** Responding; **Understand:** Using Vocabulary—amazing (I would love to visit the Great Barrier Reef. It would be amazing to see all the different kinds of animals . . .)

CHAPTER 2 INSTRUCTIONS

Students read without the teacher, independently or with partners.
Note: If you're working on an 8- to 11-Day Plan, you will read Chapter 2 with students.

COMPREHENSION PROCESSES

Remember, Understand, Apply, Analyze

PROCEDURES FOR READING ON YOUR OWN

1. Getting Ready

Identifying—Title

Have students turn to Chapter 2 on page 14.
Have students read the chapter title. Say something like:
Like all habitats, the reef has many food chains.

2. Setting a Purpose

Explaining—Facts; Using Vocabulary—coral reef, herbivore, carnivore; Defining and Using Vocabulary—omnivore

Before students begin reading, say something like:
Read to find out the answers to these questions:

- What is an example of a coral reef food chain?
- What herbivore is found on the coral reef?
- What carnivore is found on the coral reef?
- What is an omnivore?

> **PREP NOTE**
> **Setting a Purpose**
> Write questions on a chalkboard, white board, or large piece of paper before working with your small group.

3. Reading on Your Own: Partner or Whisper Reading

- Have students take turns reading every other page with a partner or have students whisper read on their own.
- Continue having students track each word with their fingers.
- Have students ask themselves or their partners the gray text questions.

For Whisper Reading, say something like:
Everyone, turn to page 14. You're going to read Chapter 2 on your own. Please whisper read with your finger, so I can see where you are in your work. Remember to ask yourself the gray text questions.

For Partner Reading, say something like:
Everyone, turn to page 14. This is where you're going to start Partner Reading.
Where are you going to sit? (at our desks, side by side)
You will take turns reading pages. If you are the listener, what will you do? (keep my book flat, follow with my finger, ask my partner the gray text questions, compliment my partner)
If you are the reader, what will you do? (keep my book flat, finger track, read quietly)
Turn to page 19. That's where you are going to stop reading.

4. Comprehension and Skill Work

For students on a 6-Day Plan, tell them they will do Comprehension and Skill Activities 1 and 2 after they read on their own. Guide practice, as needed. For teacher directions, see pages 34 and 35. (For 8- to 11-Day Plans, see the Lesson Planner, page 9.)

5. Homework 1: Repeated Reading

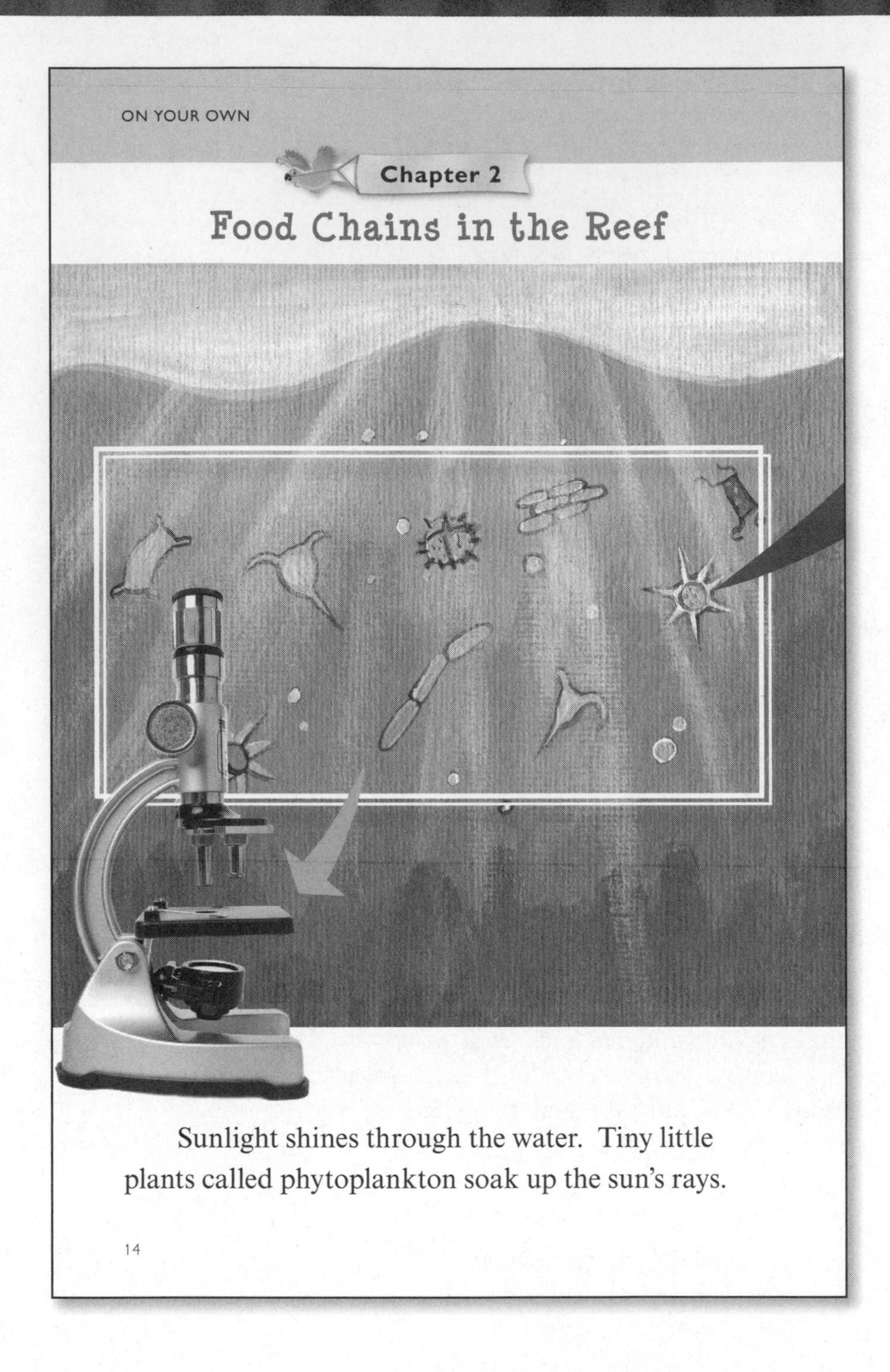

ON YOUR OWN

Chapter 2

Food Chains in the Reef

Sunlight shines through the water. Tiny little plants called phytoplankton soak up the sun's rays.

14

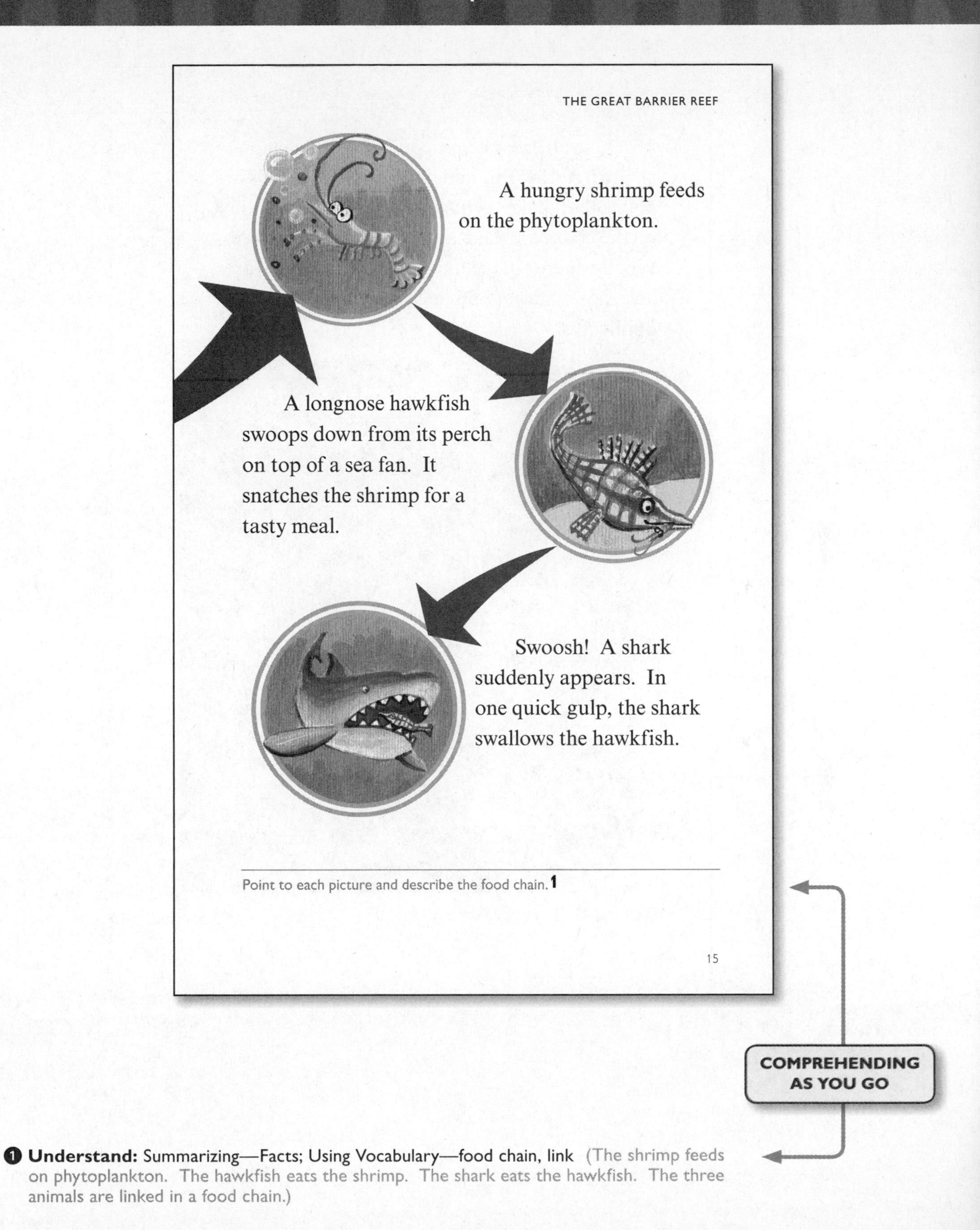

❶ **Understand:** Summarizing—Facts; Using Vocabulary—food chain, link (The shrimp feeds on phytoplankton. The hawkfish eats the shrimp. The shark eats the hawkfish. The three animals are linked in a food chain.)

ON YOUR OWN

Like all ecosystems, coral reefs have many food chains. At the beginning of these food chains are plants that make their own food from the sun. Next on the chain are the plant eaters—the herbivores. Finally, there are the meat eaters—the carnivores—and those that eat both meat and plants—the omnivores.

What does an omnivore eat? [1]

16

COMPREHENDING AS YOU GO

❶ **Remember:** Defining and Using Vocabulary—omnivore (An omnivore is an animal that eats both meat and plants.)

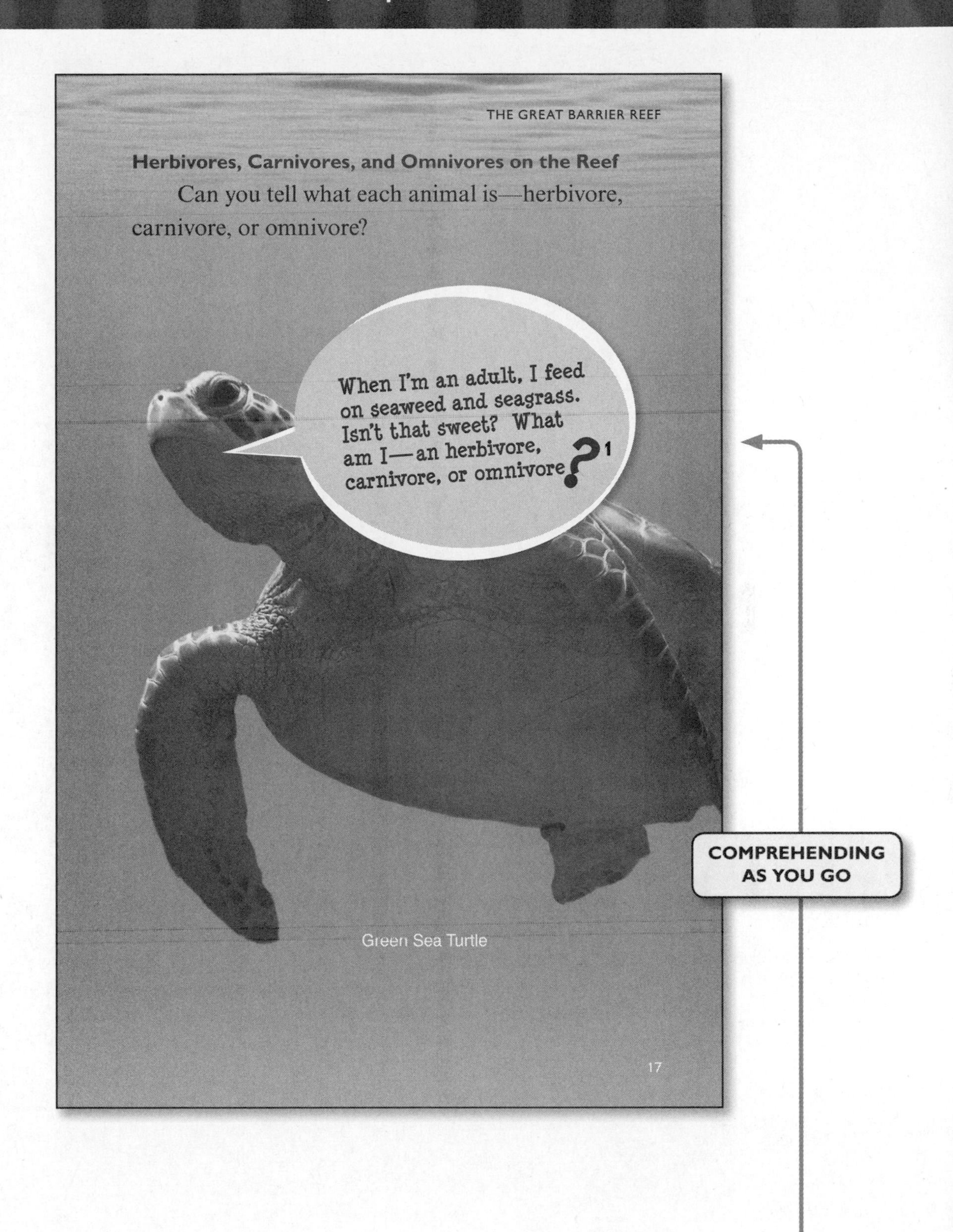

Green Sea Turtle

❶ **Analyze:** Classifying; **Apply:** Using Vocabulary—herbivore (The green sea turtle is an herbivore.)

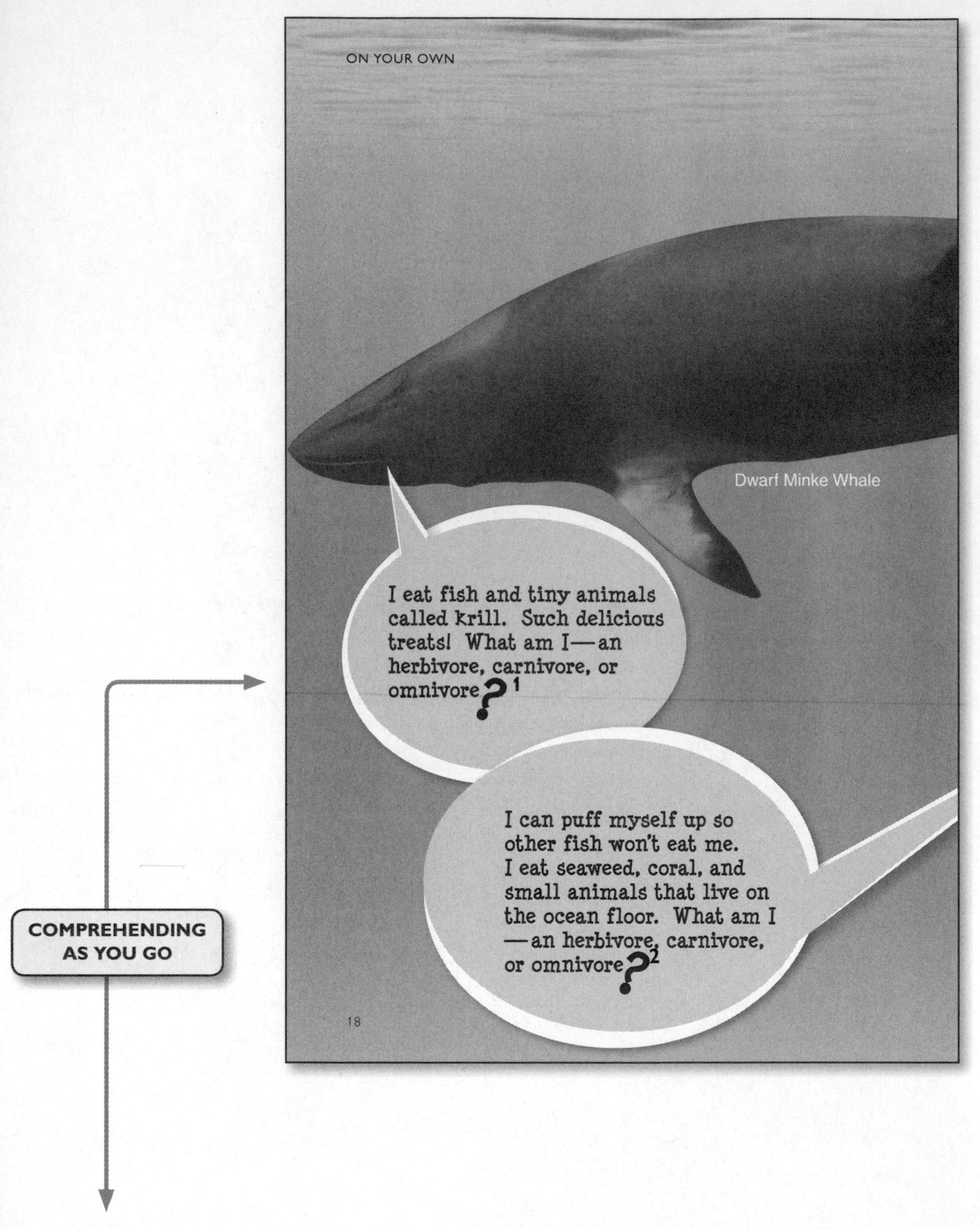

❶ **Analyze:** Classifying; **Apply:** Using Vocabulary—carnivore (The dwarf minke whale is a carnivore.)

❷ **Analyze:** Classifying **Apply:** Using Vocabulary—omnivore (The starry pufferfish is an omnivore.)

THE GREAT BARRIER REEF

Starry Pufferfish

The Reef Community

Who are we? We are members of the Great Barrier Reef community. We depend on each other.

19

PASSAGE COMPREHENSION

COMPREHENSION PROCESSES

Remember, Understand, Apply

WRITING TRAITS

Conventions—Complete Sentence, Capital, Period
Presentation

Viewing; Inferring; Explaining
Using Vocabulary—planet

Defining; Using Vocabulary—continent, coral reef

Using Vocabulary—ecosystem

Locating Information
Identifying—What
Using Vocabulary—approximately

Defining and Using Vocabulary—approximately

The Great Barrier Reef

Unit 18 Activity 1
Use after Exercise 1 and Chapters 1 and 2

Name ____________________

Passage Comprehension
The Great Barrier Reef

(Accept any reasonable response.)
1. **Open your storybook to page 9. Look at the photo of Earth from space. Why is Earth called the blue planet?**
Earth is called the blue planet because there is so much water covering it. Earth looks blue from space.

2. **The Great Barrier Reef is . . .**
○ an island. ○ a continent. ● hundreds of coral reefs and islands.

3. **An ecosystem is a community of animals and plants living together.**
The Great Barrier Reef is an example of an ecosystem.

4. **Complete the captions below.** The Great Barrier Reef is home to . . .

about 1,500 types of fish	(around) 5,000 types of mollusks	(approximately) 360 types of hard coral

5. **A snazzy word for *about* and *around* is** approximately.

61

PROCEDURES

1. **Sentence Writing—Specific Instructions** (Item 1)
Have students read the question and write a complete sentence. Tell them to start their sentence with what the question is about. The word is underlined. Say something like:
What's the question about? (Earth)
Start your answer with the word *Earth*.
Remind students to start sentences with a capital and end with a period.

2. **Selection Response—Basic Instructions** (Item 2)
Have students read the sentence starter, then fill in the bubble with the correct answer.

3. **Sentence Completion—Specific Instructions** (Items 3, 5)
Have students fill in the blank with the correct vocabulary word.

4. **Caption Completion—Specific Instructions** (Item 4)
   - Have students read the directions, then fill in the blank to complete the captions. Remind students that they can look back in their book.
   - Have students circle the two words in the captions that mean "about."

Self-monitoring
Have students check and correct their work.

PASSAGE COMPREHENSION

COMPREHENSION PROCESSES

Remember, Understand

WRITING TRAITS

Conventions—Period

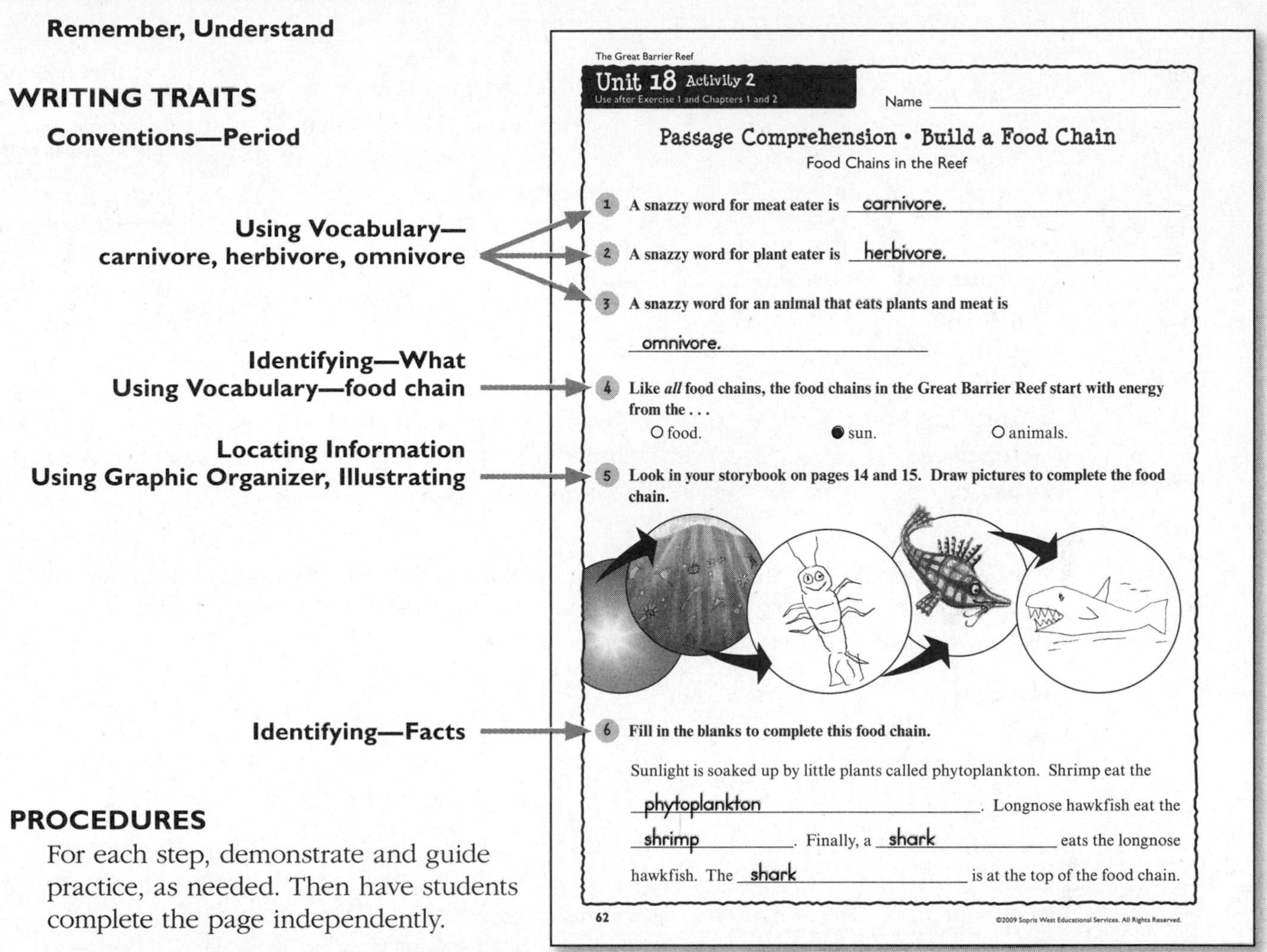

The Great Barrier Reef

Unit 18 Activity 2
Use after Exercise 1 and Chapters 1 and 2

Name ________________

Passage Comprehension • Build a Food Chain
Food Chains in the Reef

1. A snazzy word for meat eater is carnivore.
2. A snazzy word for plant eater is herbivore.
3. A snazzy word for an animal that eats plants and meat is omnivore.
4. Like *all* food chains, the food chains in the Great Barrier Reef start with energy from the . . .
   - ○ food. ● sun. ○ animals.
5. Look in your storybook on pages 14 and 15. Draw pictures to complete the food chain.
6. Fill in the blanks to complete this food chain.

Sunlight is soaked up by little plants called phytoplankton. Shrimp eat the phytoplankton. Longnose hawkfish eat the shrimp. Finally, a shark eats the longnose hawkfish. The shark is at the top of the food chain.

62

PROCEDURES

For each step, demonstrate and guide practice, as needed. Then have students complete the page independently.

1. **Vocabulary: Sentence Completion—Basic Instructions** (Items 1–3)
   Have students read the sentence starters, then fill in the blanks with the correct vocabulary word. Remind students to put a period at the end of each sentence.

2. **Selection Response—Basic Instructions** (Item 4)
   Have students read the sentence starter, then fill in the bubble with the correct answer.

3. **Diagram: Illustration—Specific Instructions** (Item 5)
   Have students draw two pictures to complete the food chain.

4. **Sentence Completion—Specific Instructions** (Item 6)
   Have students read the paragraph, then fill in the blanks with the correct answers.

Self-monitoring
Have students check and correct their work.

BUILDING INDEPENDENCE (Reminder)

For each step, demonstrate and guide practice, only as needed.
- **Demonstrate:** Have students orally answer the items while you demonstrate how to complete the page.
- **Guide:** Have students orally answer the items, but do not demonstrate how to complete the page.
- **Independent With Support:** Have students silently read over the items and ask any questions they may have.

❶ SOUND REVIEW

Have students read the sounds and key word phrases. Work for accuracy, then fluency.

❷ ACCURACY AND FLUENCY BUILDING

BUILD ACCURACY AND FLUENCY (Reminder)
For all rows and columns, follow the specific directions, then build accuracy and fluency with whole words.

C1. Multisyllabic Words

- For the list of words divided by syllables, have students read each syllable, then the whole word. Use the word in a sentence, as appropriate.
- For the list of whole words, build accuracy and then fluency.

scuba	Miss Tam wanted to learn how to . . . *scuba* . . . dive.
surrounded	We are all around you. You are . . . *surrounded.*
regulator	When you scuba dive, you breathe air through a . . . *regulator.*
vanilla	My favorite ice cream flavor is . . . *vanilla.*
moray eel	One of the animals of the Great Barrier Reef is the . . . *moray eel.*
manta ray	Another animal of the Great Barrier Reef is the . . . *manta ray.*
octopuses	Creatures with eight tentacles that can get into small cracks are . . . *octopuses.*
sausage	For breakfast, Mom is frying eggs and . . . *sausage.*

D1. Tricky Words

- For each Tricky Word, have students use the sounds and word parts they know to silently sound out the word. Use the word in a sentence to help with pronunciation.
- If the word is unfamiliar, tell students the word.

leisurely
Look at the first word. Say the word parts silently. Thumbs up when you know the word.
Use my sentence to help you pronounce the word. Devon took his time working.
He worked . . . *leisurely.* Read the word three times. (leisurely, leisurely, leisurely)

anemones
Say the word parts silently. Thumbs up when you know the word. Use my sentence to help you pronounce the word. The tide pool was full of colorful sea . . . *anemones.*
Read the word three times. (anemones, anemones, anemones)

gradually	The seeds didn't grow into plants overnight. They grew . . . *gradually.*
pudding	For dessert, I love to eat chocolate . . . *pudding.*
pears	My favorite fruits are apples and . . . *pears.*
worth	How much is that expensive diamond ring . . . *worth?*
luscious	That dessert was scrumptious. It was . . . *luscious.*

- Have students go back and read the whole words in the column.

❸ COMPOUND WORDS

❹ MORPHOGRAPHS AND AFFIXES

★In Row A, introduce and practice the affix *-ness.* Say something like:
You can already read your new affix. Sound it out. (/ness/, -ness) What does the affix say? (-ness)
Read the underlined affix and then each whole word. (-ness, fairness . . .)

- In Row B, have students read each affix and then the whole word. For the words "rereading" and "review," review the meaning of the morphograph *re-.*
- Repeat practice with whole words, mixing group and individual turns.
Build accuracy, then fluency.

★= New in this unit

❺ GENERALIZATION: READING NEW WORDS IN PARAGRAPHS

- Have students read the paragraph silently, then out loud. Tell students to use the sounds and word parts they know to read any difficult words.
- Repeat practice, as needed.

Unit 18 Exercise 2

Use before Chapters 1 and 2

1. SOUND REVIEW Have students review sounds for accuracy, then for fluency.

A	oo as in moon	ow as in cow	a as in ago	ea as in eagle	oo as in book
B	or	o_e	ai	ch	ar

2. ACCURACY/FLUENCY BUILDING For each column, have students say any underlined part, then read each word. Next, have them read the column.

A1 Mixed Practice	B1 Word Endings	C1 Multisyllabic Words		D1 Tricky Words
Aussie	fluttering	scu•ba	scuba	leisurely
budge	bellowed	sur•round•ed	surrounded	anemones
waist	mumbled	reg•u•la•tor	regulator	gradually
orange	rubbery	va•nil•la	vanilla	pudding
hoses	bobbing	mor•ay eel	moray eel	pears
phew	inflate	man•ta ray	manta ray	worth
sorted	inflatable	oc•to•pus•es	octopuses	luscious
guided		sau•sage	sausage	

3. COMPOUND WORDS Have students read the words.

parrotfish	pufferfish	halfway	wetsuit

4. MORPHOGRAPHS AND AFFIXES Have students practice reading "-ness" and the related words. For Row B, have students read the underlined part, then the word.

A	★-ness	fairness	kindness	neatness	darkness
B	heavily	instructions	position	rereading	review

5. GENERALIZATION Have students read the paragraph silently, then out loud. (New words: penguin, nonetheless, instructor, hooly-dooly)

April was getting ready for her first dive off the coast of Australia. Her suit was so tight she waddled like a penguin as she moved to the side of the boat. Nonetheless, she was ready to go as her instructor motioned for her to jump. "Hooly-dooly!" April yelled as she jumped into the waters of the Great Barrier Reef.

KEEP LESSONS MOVING WITH FINGER TRACKING

Always require finger tracking. This will:
- prevent having to stop to help students find their places.
- ensure students are practicing even when it's someone else's turn.
- allow you to monitor on-task behavior.
- increase focus and accuracy.

COMPREHENSION PROCESSES

Remember, Understand, Apply

PROCEDURES

1. Reviewing Chapter 2 (The Great Barrier Reef)

Viewing; Summarizing—Facts; Using Vocabulary—coral reef, herbivore, carnivore; Defining and Using Vocabulary—omnivore

Have students turn to page 14. Quickly review what they learned about the questions from Chapter 2, Setting a Purpose. Say something like:

Turn to page 14. Yesterday, you read Chapter 2 of "The Great Barrier Reef" on your own.

Let's see what you found out about food chains on the reef.

What is an example of a coral reef food chain? (A shrimp eats phytoplankton, then a hawkfish eats the shrimp, then a shark eats the hawkfish.)

What herbivore is found on the coral reef? (A green sea turtle is found on the coral reef.)

What carnivore is found on the coral reef? (A dwarf minke whale is found on the coral reef.)

What is an omnivore? (An omnivore is an animal that eats meat and plants.)

2. Introducing the Story

Using the Table of Contents; Identifying—Title; Predicting

Have students identify the second story in the Table of Contents, then turn to the title page.

Today, we're going to read another story about the reef.

What's the title of your new story? (Miss Tam at the Great Barrier Reef)

What do you think Miss Tam is going to do in this story? (She's going to go on another trip. She's going to go to the Great Barrier Reef.)

Everyone, what page should we turn to? (page 20)

Table of Contents

UNIT 18 • The Reef

2

3. Introducing the Title Page

Have students look at the picture and discuss the gray text questions. Say something like:

I'm happy to see Miss Tam return. She's gotten to be like an old friend.

❶ **Apply:** Inferring, Explaining (Miss Tam put the bright pink hatpin on the Great Barrier Reef.)

COMPREHENSION PROCESSES

Understand, Apply

PROCEDURES

1. Introducing Vocabulary

★inflatable ★regulator
★leisurely ★review

- For each vocabulary word, have students read the word by parts, then read the whole word.
- Read the student-friendly explanations to students as they follow with their fingers. Then have students use the vocabulary word by following the gray text.
- Review and discuss the photos.

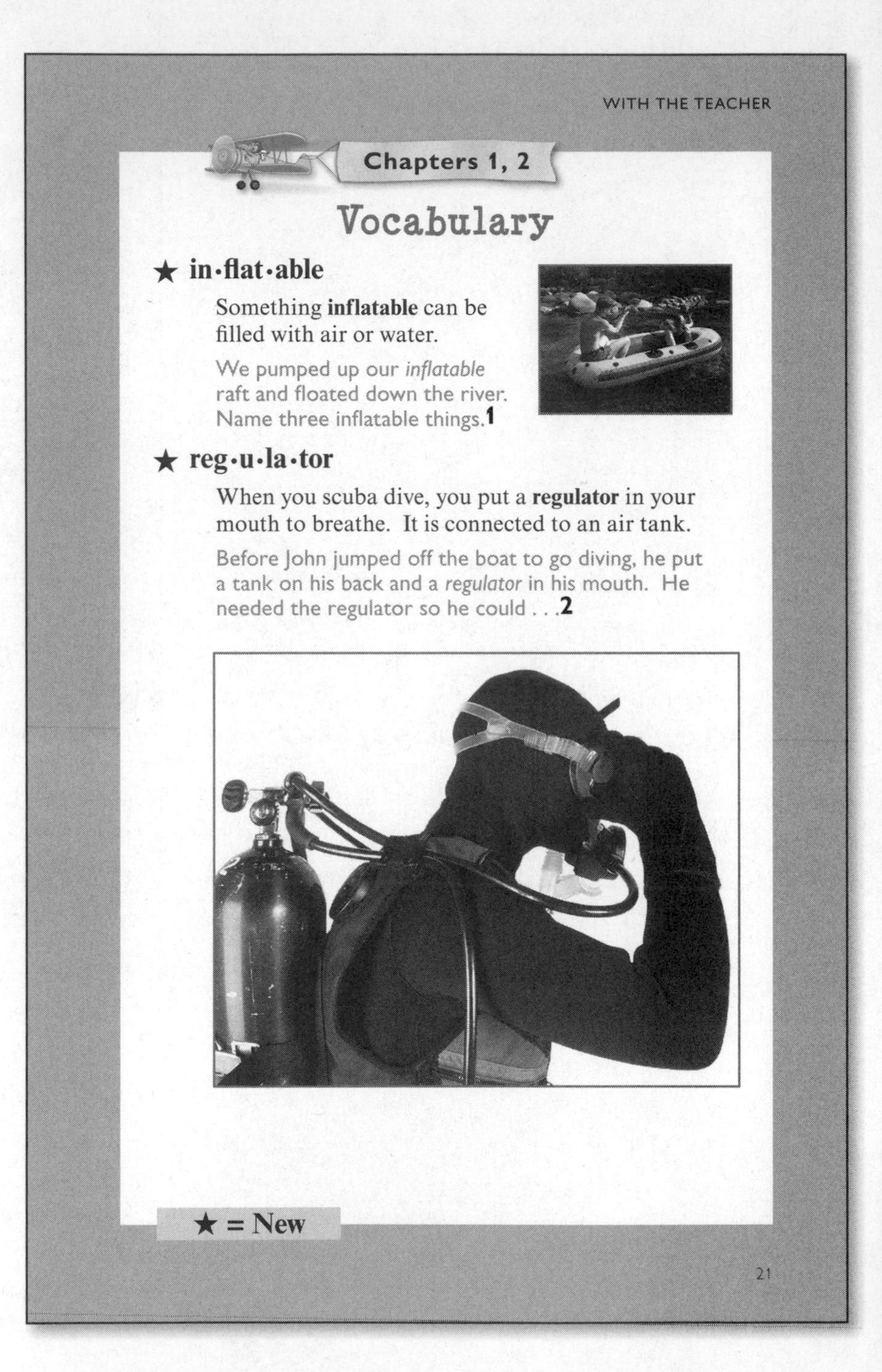

WITH THE TEACHER

Chapters 1, 2

Vocabulary

★ **in•flat•able**

Something **inflatable** can be filled with air or water.

We pumped up our *inflatable* raft and floated down the river. Name three inflatable things.1

★ **reg•u•la•tor**

When you scuba dive, you put a **regulator** in your mouth to breathe. It is connected to an air tank.

Before John jumped off the boat to go diving, he put a tank on his back and a *regulator* in his mouth. He needed the regulator so he could . . .2

★ = New

21

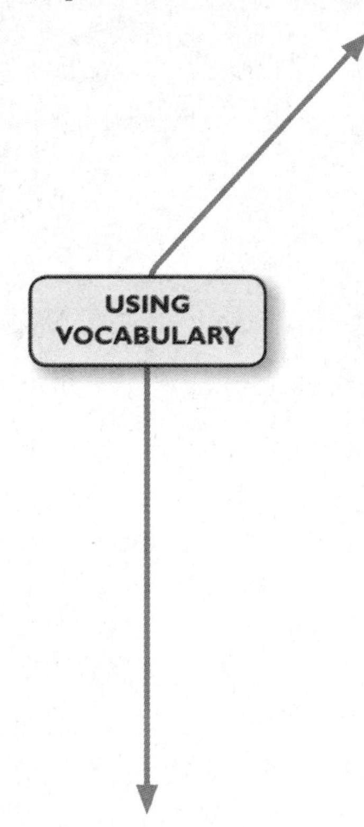

❶ **Apply:** Using Vocabulary—inflatable (A beach ball, an inner tube, and a raft are inflatable things.)

❷ **Apply:** Using Vocabulary—regulator (breathe)

★= New in this unit

2. Now You Try It!

- Read or paraphrase the directions.
- Have students read the word by parts, then read the whole word.
- Have students explain or define the word in their own words. Say something like:

  Look at the word. Say the parts, then read the whole word.

  (re•view, review)

  Now let's pretend that we're going to explain or define the word *review* to a friend. [Samantha], what would you say?

  Start with "*Review* means to . . . " (Review means to go back over something.)

  That's right. Review means to go back over something you've already looked at or studied.

- Have students turn to the appropriate page in the glossary and discuss how their definition is the same as or different from the glossary's. Your students may like their definition better.

Note: By defining a word in their own words, students are demonstrating depth of word knowledge. Verbatim responses only demonstrate memorization. Encourage paraphrasing.

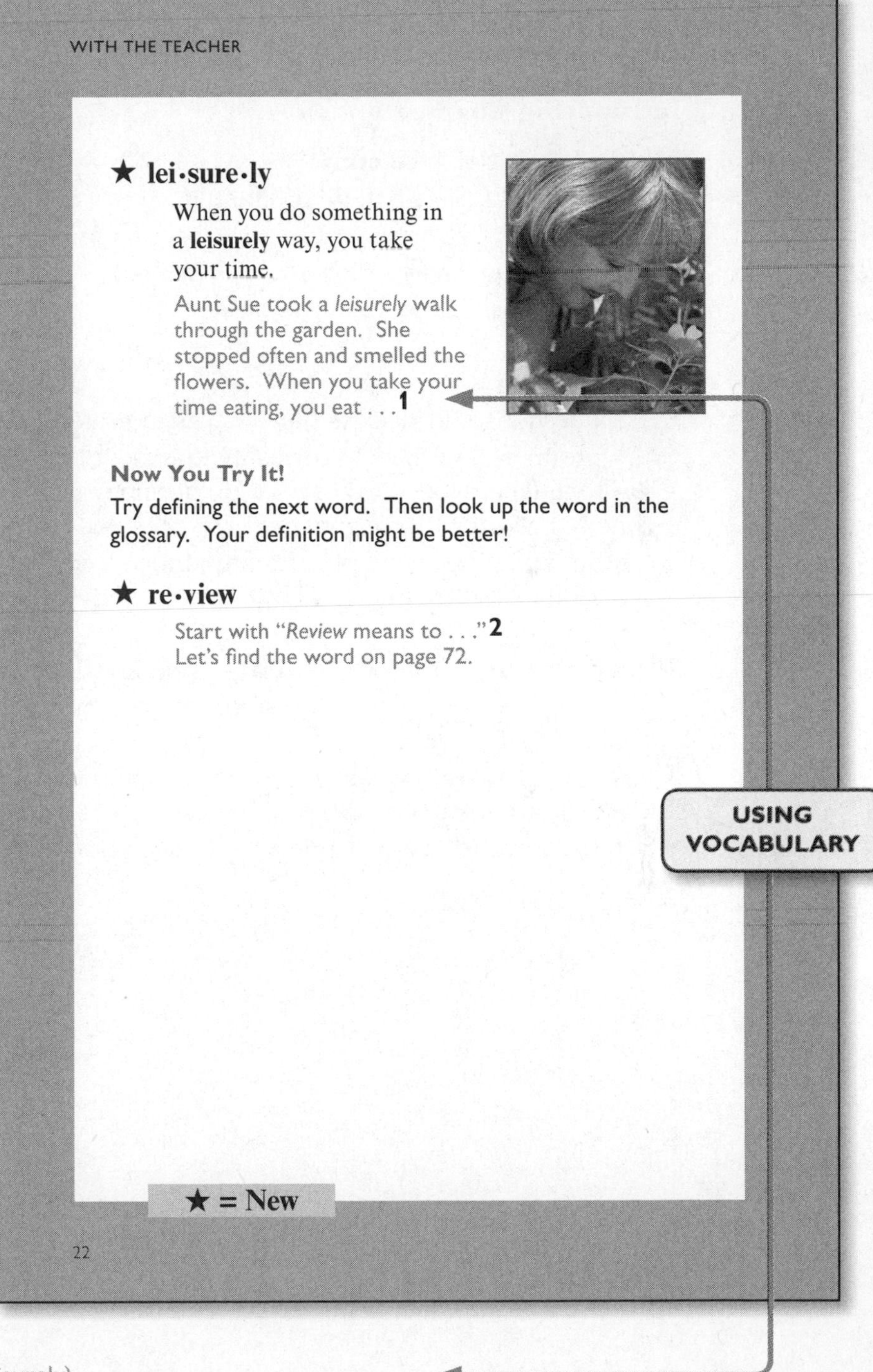

WITH THE TEACHER

★ **lei•sure•ly**

When you do something in a **leisurely** way, you take your time.

Aunt Sue took a *leisurely* walk through the garden. She stopped often and smelled the flowers. When you take your time eating, you eat . . . **1**

Now You Try It!

Try defining the next word. Then look up the word in the glossary. Your definition might be better!

★ **re•view**

Start with "*Review* means to . . ."**2**
Let's find the word on page 72.

★ = New

22

❶ **Apply:** Using Vocabulary—leisurely (leisurely)

❷ **Understand:** Defining and Using Vocabulary—review; Using Glossary (Review means to go back over something you've already looked at or studied.)

CHAPTER 1 INSTRUCTIONS

Students read Chapter 1 with the teacher and Chapter 2 on their own.

COMPREHENSION PROCESSES

Remember, Understand, Apply

PROCEDURES

1. Introducing Chapter 1

Identifying—Title; Predicting

Discuss the title. Say something like:

Turn to page 23. What's the title of the first chapter? (Suiting Up)

What do you think might happen in this chapter?

(Miss Tam is going to get ready for a dive.)

2. First Reading

- Ask questions and discuss the story as indicated by the gray text.
- Mix group and individual turns, independent of your voice. Have students work toward a group accuracy goal of 0–5 errors. Quietly keep track of errors made by all students in the group.
- After reading the story, practice any difficult words. Reread the story if students have not reached the accuracy goal.

3. Second Reading, Timed Readings: Repeated Reading

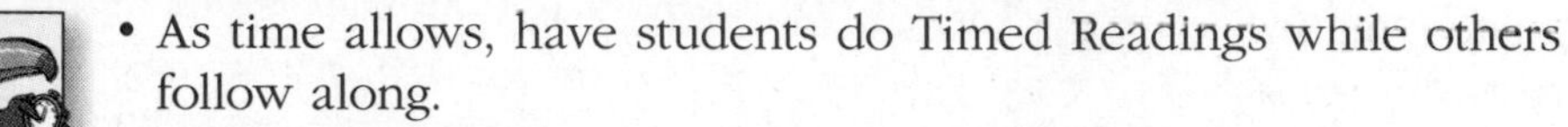

- As time allows, have students do Timed Readings while others follow along.
- Time individuals for 30 seconds and encourage each child to work for a personal best.
- Determine words correct per minute. Record student scores.

Chapter 1

Suiting Up

Miss Tam sat in a big boat off the coast of Australia. Water glistened in every direction.

Miss Tam was very excited. Today would be her first dive. She couldn't wait to see the giant clams, clownfish, eels, and, of course, pufferfish and octopuses. Miss Tam smiled. "Here I come—Miss Tam to the Great Barrier Reef."

The dive instructor handed Miss Tam a black rubbery suit. "Oh my," said Miss Tam as she looked at the suit. It seemed a bit small. Nonetheless, she stuck her feet through the leg holes and tried to pull the suit up her legs. It wouldn't budge!

Where is Miss Tam? **1** What is she going to do? **2**

COMPREHENDING AS YOU GO

❶ **Remember:** Identifying—Setting; Using Vocabulary—Australia (Miss Tam is at the Great Barrier Reef off the coast of Australia.)

❷ **Apply:** Inferring; Explaining (Miss Tam is going scuba diving so she is putting on a wetsuit.)

WITH THE TEACHER

"Oh my," thought Miss Tam. Determined, she stood up and tugged again. The suit came up to her knees and stopped. Miss Tam sighed and looked around. Right–left, right–left, people were dancing from foot to foot as they wiggled into their wetsuits. Miss Tam thought the dance was worth a try.

Right, tug, left, tug. Finally, the tight black suit was up as far as her waist. "Phew!" said Miss Tam.

The instructor smiled at Miss Tam. "Good on ya, mate! You're halfway there," he said. In her best Aussie English, Miss Tam mumbled, "Ah, good on us."

Why were people dancing from foot to foot?[1] Why did Miss Tam's instructor say, "Good on ya, mate"?[2]

24

COMPREHENDING AS YOU GO

❶ **Apply:** Inferring, Explaining (Wetsuits are tight and difficult to put on. Dancing from foot to foot helps you wiggle into the suit.)

❷ **Apply:** Inferring, Explaining (The instructor was encouraging Miss Tam to keep trying until she got her suit on. It's like saying, "Good job.")

Miss Tam watched as others on the boat began a second dance. Left–right, left–right . . . Miss Tam leaned over and pushed her left hand down its sleeve, then right–left–right, until, finally, her hands reached air. "Phew!" said Miss Tam as she wiggled and bent her fingers to make sure she could still feel them.

Just as she thought she was ready—zip! Her instructor closed up the back of her wetsuit. "Oh my," thought Miss Tam, but she couldn't say a thing. The suit was so tight she felt like a stuffed sausage.

Why did Miss Tam feel like a stuffed sausage? 1

COMPREHENDING AS YOU GO

1 **Understand:** Explaining (Her wetsuit was very tight. She felt like she was stuffed into it.)

But there was more! Miss Tam had to strap a 10-pound weight belt around her waist. Then the instructor helped her into an inflatable vest that held a 30-pound tank of air. Next, they sorted through the tangle of hoses so everything was in its right position. Finally, the instructor went through the safety check and reviewed the dive instructions.

With the safety check done, Miss Tam sat down heavily on a wooden bench. She carefully put her face mask over her eyes and nose so it wouldn't leak. She was ready. "Great Barrier Reef, here I come," she thought.

SETTING

1. Where does the story take place?

GOAL

2. Why did Miss Tam go to the Great Barrier Reef?

PREDICTION

3. What do you think Miss Tam will see?

PERSONAL RESPONSE

4. How would you feel if you were Miss Tam? Why?

❶ **Remember:** Identifying—Setting; Using Vocabulary—Australia (The story takes place in Australia at the Great Barrier Reef.)

❷ **Apply:** Inferring—Goal: **Understand:** Describing—Character Traits (Characterization); Using Vocabulary—adventure, coral reef (Miss Tam likes to travel. She likes adventure. She wanted to see the giant clams, clownfish, eels, pufferfish, and octopuses. She wanted to see a coral reef.)

❸ **Apply:** Predicting (Miss Tam will see lots of colorful fish. She'll see a pufferfish and an octopus . . .)

❹ **Evaluate:** Responding (I would feel excited. I think I would be nervous. I would want to get in the water . . .)

CHAPTER 2 INSTRUCTIONS

Students read without the teacher, independently or with partners.

COMPREHENSION PROCESSES

Remember, Understand, Apply

PROCEDURES FOR READING ON YOUR OWN

1. Getting Ready

Have students turn to Chapter 2 on page 28.

2. Setting a Purpose

Explaining

Before students begin reading, say something like:

As you read the next pages, try to answer:

- What does it sound like when you talk with a regulator in your mouth?
- What did Miss Tam feel like underwater?
- What did Miss Tam see on her dive at the coral reef?

PREP NOTE
Setting a Purpose
Write questions on a chalkboard, white board, or large piece of paper before working with your small group.

3. Reading on Your Own: Partner or Whisper Reading

- Have students take turns reading every other page with a partner or have students whisper read on their own.
- Continue having students track each word with their fingers.
- Have students ask themselves or their partners the gray text questions.

4. Comprehension and Skill Work

For students on a 6-Day Plan, tell them they will do Comprehension and Skill Activities 3 and 4 after they read on their own. Guide practice, as needed. For teacher directions, see pages 54 and 55. (For 8- to 11-Day Plans, see the Lesson Planner, page 9.)

5. Homework 2: Repeated Reading

Jumping In

Suddenly, the dive instructor bellowed, "Time to get wet!"

Miss Tam waddled like a penguin toward the gate on the side of the boat. She held onto the side of the boat as she tugged on one big pink fin at a time. She stood at the gate, put her regulator in her mouth, and took a deep breath.

The instructor was waiting in the clear blue water. He motioned to Miss Tam. Miss Tam put one bright pink foot forward. "Oh my," she said. Through her regulator it sounded more like "Mmm mmm." Then Miss Tam jumped feet-first into the deep blue ocean.

Once she was in the water, Miss Tam's inflatable vest kept her bobbing on the surface while she breathed rapidly through her regulator. The instructor motioned for her to let the air out of her vest. Within seconds, Miss Tam and her instructor were sinking into the ocean. Nervous but excited, Miss Tam thought, "Parrotfish, giant clams . . . Great Barrier Reef, here I come!"

Surrounded by water, Miss Tam gradually relaxed. With a flip of her fin, she glided through the ocean water. Miss Tam thought, "I feel like a fish." A six-foot moray eel swam by. Miss Tam thought, "Well, I'll be." Then she remembered her best Aussie English and tried to say "hooly-dooly" to her dive instructor. Through the regulator, it came out "oody-oody!"

On the boat, Miss Tam felt like a penguin. Why? [1] Now that she's in the water, Miss Tam feels like a fish. Why? [2]

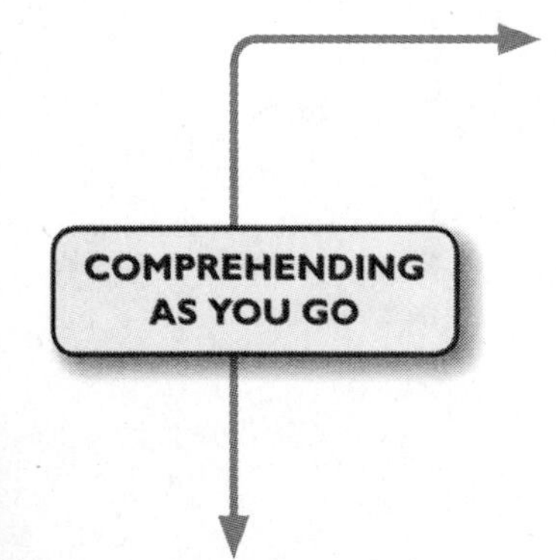

❶ **Apply:** Inferring, Explaining (In the wetsuit, she could only waddle—like a penguin on land.)

❷ **Apply:** Inferring; Explaining (She has fins on her feet so she can glide through the water—just like a fish.)

Miss Tam's dive instructor carefully guided her around the reef. The coral was so colorful! Miss Tam was amazed. She wanted to reach out and touch the waving sea fans, the funny fat pufferfish, and the huge plates of coral, but she was very careful not to touch anything. Striped angelfish swam nearby, little orange and white clownfish looked up at her from the sea anemones, and a huge twelve-foot manta ray swept past above her.

❶ **Understand:** Describing; Using Vocabulary—coral reef (Miss Tam saw a six-foot moray eel and a colorful coral reef. She saw waving sea fans, funny fat pufferfish, striped angelfish, and orange and white clownfish. She also saw a huge manta ray.)

That evening, Miss Tam sat in her hotel room. After finishing a luscious lemon rice pudding with pears and vanilla ice cream, she settled in for a leisurely rereading of a book about the Great Barrier Reef. Miss Tam opened the book. Colorful coral, graceful fish fluttering through the coral, a spotted eel staring right out of the page . . . Miss Tam thought, "Oh my. It is a wonder!" Then, before she knew it, she was snoring. It had been an eventful day on the Great Barrier Reef!

What did Miss Tam eat after her dive? **1** Why was it an *eventful* day? **2** Why do you think Miss Tam ordered rice pudding? **3**

COMPREHENDING AS YOU GO

❶ **Remember:** Identifying—What (Miss Tam ate lemon rice pudding with pears and vanilla ice cream.)

❷ **Apply:** Inferring; Explaining; Using Vocabulary—eventful (It was eventful because many special things happened. Miss Tam learned how to put on a wetsuit and all the other diving gear, and she saw many incredible animals at the Great Barrier Reef.)

❸ **Apply:** Inferring; Explaining; Using Vocabulary—habit (Miss Tam is a person of habit. She eats rice wherever she goes.)

STORY COMPREHENSION

COMPREHENSION PROCESSES

Remember, Understand, Apply, Evaluate, Create

WRITING TRAITS

Ideas and Content
Word Choice
Conventions—Complete Sentence, Capital, Period
Presentation

Explaining—Setting

Identifying—What

Responding, Generating Ideas Sentence Writing

Using Graphic Organizer; Identifying—What; Using Vocabulary—inflatable

Miss Tam at The Great Barrier Reef

Unit 18 Activity 3
Use after Exercise 2 and Chapters 1 and 2

Name ____________________

Story Comprehension
Miss Tam at the Great Barrier Reef

1. **Where does the story take place?**
The story takes place at the Great Barrier Reef.

2. **It was funny to imagine Miss Tam . . .**
● squeezing into a wetsuit. ○ going to the Great Barrier Reef.
(Accept any reasonable response.)

3. **Write two or more sentences that tell what you think about Miss Tam and why.**
I like (like / do not like) Miss Tam because she likes to take trips. She likes to try new things.

4. **Look at Miss Tam. Label her diving equipment.**
The first one has been done for you.
- face mask
- weight belt
- inflatable vest
- air tank
- fins

face mask
air tank
inflatable vest
weight belt
fins

 63

PROCEDURES

For each step, demonstrate and guide practice, as needed. Then have students complete the page independently.

1. **Sentence Writing—Basic Instructions** (Item 1)
Have students read the question and write a complete sentence. Tell them to start their sentence with what the question is about. The words are underlined. Remind students to start sentences with a capital and end with a period.

2. **Selection Response—Basic Instructions** (Item 2)
Have students read the sentence starter, then fill in the bubble for the answer.

3. **Personal Response: Paragraph Writing—Specific Instructions** (Item 3)
Have students read the directions and write two or more sentences that explain how they feel about Miss Tam. Remind them to start sentences with a capital and end with period.

4. **Diagram: Labeling—Basic Instructions** (Item 4)
Have students read the directions and label Miss Tam's diving equipment, using the list provided.

Self-monitoring
Have students check and correct their work.

STORY MAP

COMPREHENSION PROCESSES

Remember, Understand

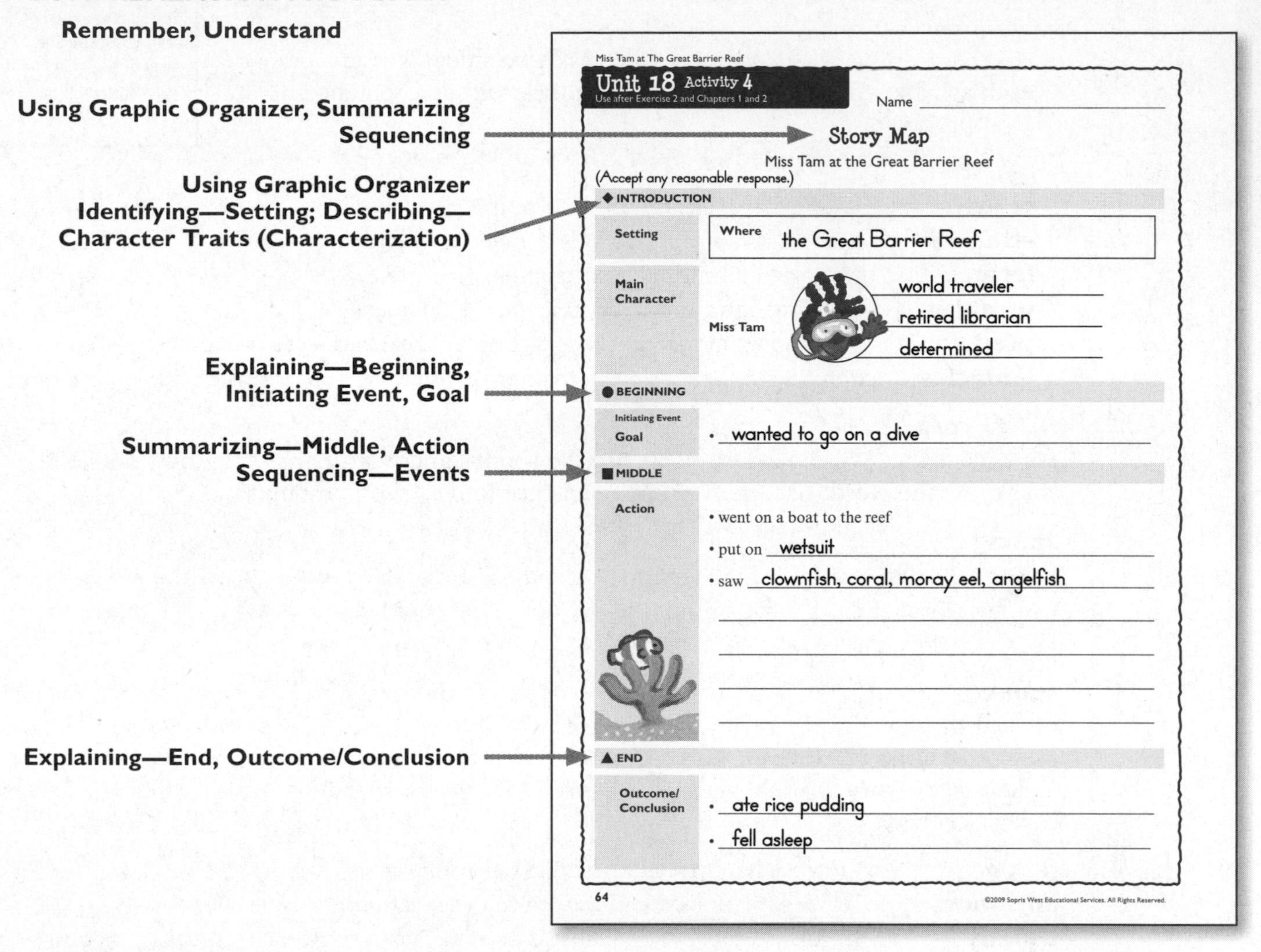

Miss Tam at The Great Barrier Reef

Unit 18 Activity 4
Use after Exercise 2 and Chapters 1 and 2

Name ____________

Story Map
Miss Tam at the Great Barrier Reef

(Accept any reasonable response.)

◆ INTRODUCTION

Setting — Where: the Great Barrier Reef

Main Character — Miss Tam: world traveler; retired librarian; determined

● BEGINNING

Initiating Event / Goal — • wanted to go on a dive

■ MIDDLE

Action
- went on a boat to the reef
- put on wetsuit
- saw clownfish, coral, moray eel, angelfish

▲ END

Outcome/Conclusion
- ate rice pudding
- fell asleep

64

©2009 Sopris West Educational Services. All Rights Reserved.

PROCEDURES

Use an overhead BLM copy of the story map to demonstrate and guide practice, only as needed.

Story Map: Character Web, Sentence Completion—Basic Instructions

- Have students complete each section of the story map: introduction, beginning, middle, and end.
- For some groups, provide students with time to complete each section before you move to the next.
- For more independent writers, have students complete the map independently.

❶ SOUND REVIEW Use selected Sound Cards from Units 1–18.

BUILD ACCURACY AND FLUENCY (Reminder)
For all rows and columns, follow the specific directions, then build accuracy and fluency with whole words.

❷ ACCURACY AND FLUENCY BUILDING

C1. Multisyllabic Words

- For the list of words divided by syllables, have students read each syllable, then the whole word. Use the word in a sentence, as appropriate.
- For the list of whole words, build accuracy and then fluency.

relative Your aunt, uncle, or cousin is your . . . *relative.*
stingers Bees have sharp pointed parts called . . . *stingers.*
lettuce My salad had cucumbers, tomatoes, and . . . *lettuce.*
mistake Christina used an eraser to fix her . . . *mistake.*
predator A sea anenome catches and eats other creatures. A sea anenome is a . . . *predator.*
tentacles Some sea creatures catch their pray with long, thin organs called . . . *tentacles.*

D1. Tricky Words

For each Tricky Word, have students use the sounds and word parts they know to silently sound out the word. Use the word in a sentence to help with pronunciation.

among
Look at the first word. Say the word parts silently. Thumbs up when you know the word. Use my sentence to help you pronounce the word. The deer hid . . . *among* . . . the trees. Read the word three times. (among, among, among)

sponge
Look at the next word. I think you can figure this Tricky Word out. Say the word parts silently, then thumbs up when you know it. Use my sentence to help. Amanda cleaned up the milk that spilled with a . . . *sponge.* There is also a sea creature called a . . . *sponge.* Read the word three times. (sponge, sponge, sponge)

polyp A tiny animal that helps to build the coral reef is the coral . . . *polyp.*
anemones The Great Barrier Reef is home to millions of sea . . . *anemones.*
usually He goes to the library almost every day. That's what he . . . *usually* . . . does.
energy Food gives you . . . *energy.*

❸ WORD ENDINGS

❹ WORDS IN CONTEXT

❺ MORPHOGRAPHS AND AFFIXES

- Remind students that a morphograph is a word part that has meaning.
- ★Introduce "less = without."
  Look at Row A. The morphograph *-less* means without. So we can say that *-less* equals without. Everyone, read that with me. *-less* equals without.
- For each word, have students read what the word means and the accompanying sentence. Have students rephrase the sentence.
  -less means without, so helpless means without help. Read the sentence.
  (The little puppy was helpless.) That means the little puppy was . . . without help.
- Repeat with "endless equals without end" and "brainless equals without a brain."
- For Row D, have students read the underlined part, then the word.

★= New in this unit

❻ GENERALIZATION: READING NEW WORDS IN PARAGRAPHS

- Have students read the paragraph silently, then out loud. Tell students to use the sounds and word parts they know to read any difficult words.
- Repeat practice, as needed.

Wonders of the Coral Reef

Unit 18 **Exercise 3**
Use before Chapters 1 and 2

1. SOUND REVIEW Use selected Sound Cards from Units 1–18.

2. ACCURACY/FLUENCY BUILDING For each column, have students say any underlined part, then read each word. Next, have them read the column.

A1 Mixed Practice	B1 Mixed Practice	C1 Multisyllabic Words		D1 Tricky Words
kinds	choices	rel•a•tive	relative	among
slug	turtle	sting•ers	stingers	sponge
tube	floating	let•tuce	lettuce	polyp
seek	yellow	mis•take	mistake	anemones
enjoy	purple	pred•a•tor	predator	usually
		ten•ta•cles	tentacles	energy

3. WORD ENDINGS Have students read any underlined word, then the word with an ending.

A	builders		twirling		diver	leafy
B	live	living	dazzle	dazzling	imagine	imagining

4. WORDS IN CONTEXT Have students use the sounds and word parts they know to figure out each word. Then have them read each sentence.

A	al•gae	A green, slimy plant that grows near or in water is algae.
B	nu•di•branch (brank)	A nudibranch is a mollusk without a shell.

5. MORPHOGRAPHS AND AFFIXES Have students practice reading "-less equals without" and the related words and sentences. For Row D, have students read the underlined part, then the word.

A	★ -less = without	helpless = without help	The little puppy was helpless.
B		endless = without end	The road seemed to be endless.
C		brainless = without a brain	The little jellyfish was brainless.
D	cleverness, division	incredible	business, fairness

6. GENERALIZATION Have students read the paragraph silently, then out loud. (New words: disguise, slithering, suckers, attached)

Guess what I am! I am a sea creature that lives in the coral reef. I protect myself by changing color. That is my disguise. I am also a shape-shifting creature, and you can find me slithering through small openings. I have eight long arms with suckers attached to them. If someone or something gets too close, I can shoot out a cloud of ink and dart away.

If you guessed I am an octopus, you are right!

45

BUILDING INDEPENDENCE (Reminder)

Some students will try to follow your voice instead of learning to read the sounds and words. Therefore, it is important for you to demonstrate and guide practice only as needed.

Give students many opportunities to respond without your assistance—with groups and individuals. Encourage independence.

COMPREHENSION PROCESSES

Remember, Understand, Apply, Analyze, Create

PROCEDURES

1. Reviewing Chapter 2 (Miss Tam at the Great Barrier Reef)

Summarizing; Using Vocabulary—coral reef

Have students turn to page 28. Quickly discuss the questions from Chapter 2, Setting a Purpose. Say something like:

Yesterday, you read Chapter 2 of "Miss Tam at the Great Barrier Reef" on your own. Let's see what you found out.

What does it sound like when you talk with a regulator in your mouth?
(It sounds like you are mumbling, like how you talk after you go to the dentist.)

What did Miss Tam feel like underwater?
(She felt like a fish.)

What did Miss Tam see on her dive at the coral reef?
(She saw coral, pufferfish, clownfish, a manta ray, sea anemones . . .)

2. Introducing the Story

Using Table of Contents; Identifying—Title; Classifying—Genre

Have students identify the third story in the unit. Then turn to the title page.

Today, we're going to read another story about the reef.

What's the title of your new story?
(Wonders of the Coral Reef.)

Is the story fiction or nonfiction?
(nonfiction)

Everyone, what page should we turn to? (page 33)

TABLE OF CONTENTS

UNIT 18 • The Reef

2

3. Introducing the Title Page
Discuss the title page and the gray text questions.

❶ **Apply:** Priming Background Knowledge; Using Vocabulary—coral reef, food chain (A coral reef is alive. A coral reef has many food chains.)

❷ **Create:** Generating Ideas, Asking Questions (What animals build coral reefs? What are the reefs made of? Why are they colorful . . .)

COMPREHENSION PROCESSES

Understand, Apply

PROCEDURES

1. Introducing Vocabulary

★coral polyp ★algae ★nudibranch, colony

- For each vocabulary word, have students read the word by parts, then read the whole word.
- Read the student-friendly explanations to students as they follow with their fingers. Then have students use the vocabulary word by following the gray text.
- Review and discuss the photos.

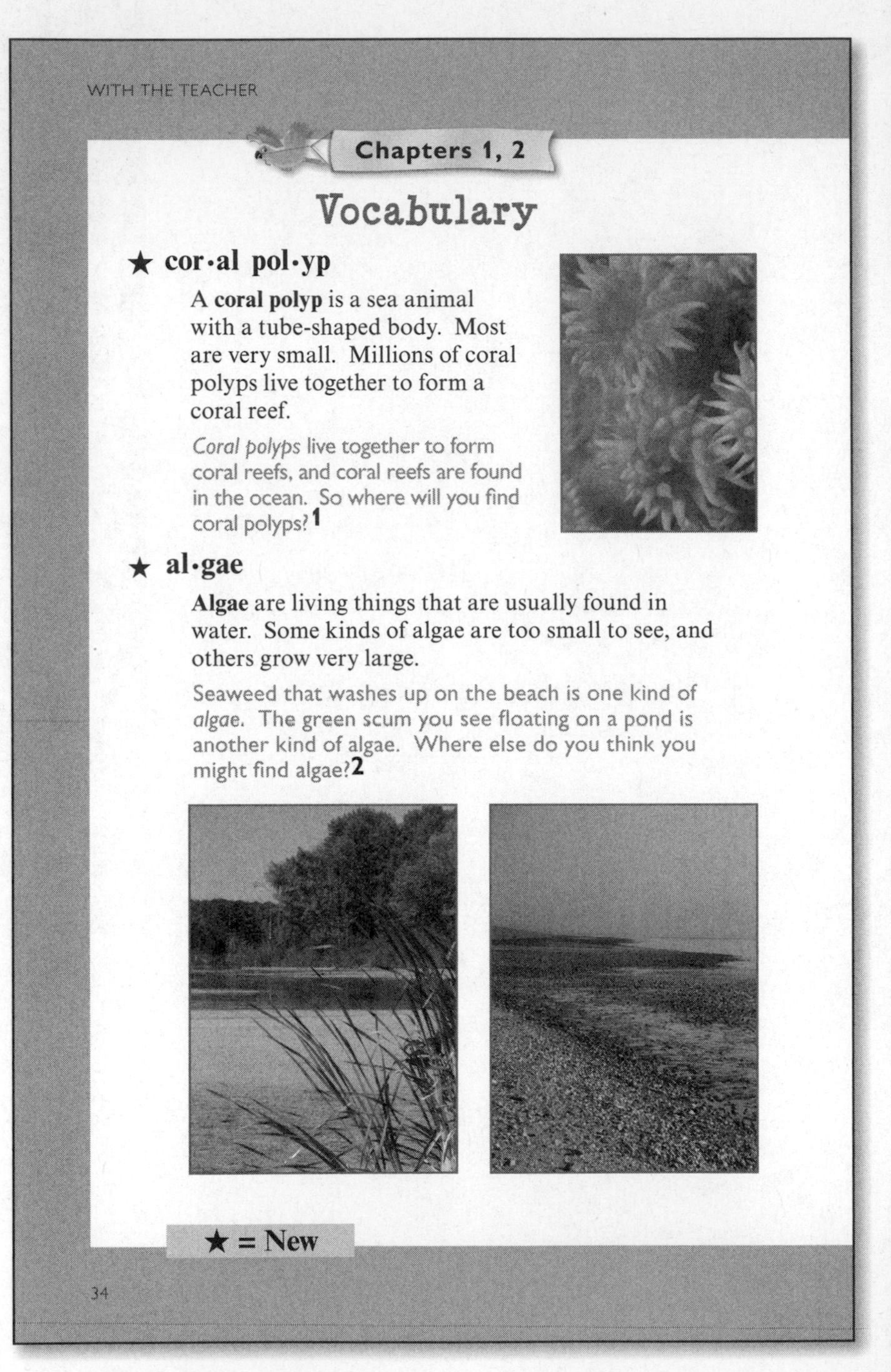

WITH THE TEACHER

Chapters 1, 2

Vocabulary

★ **cor•al pol•yp**

A **coral polyp** is a sea animal with a tube-shaped body. Most are very small. Millions of coral polyps live together to form a coral reef.

Coral polyps live together to form coral reefs, and coral reefs are found in the ocean. So where will you find coral polyps?1

★ **al•gae**

Algae are living things that are usually found in water. Some kinds of algae are too small to see, and others grow very large.

Seaweed that washes up on the beach is one kind of *algae*. The green scum you see floating on a pond is another kind of algae. Where else do you think you might find algae?2

★ = New

34

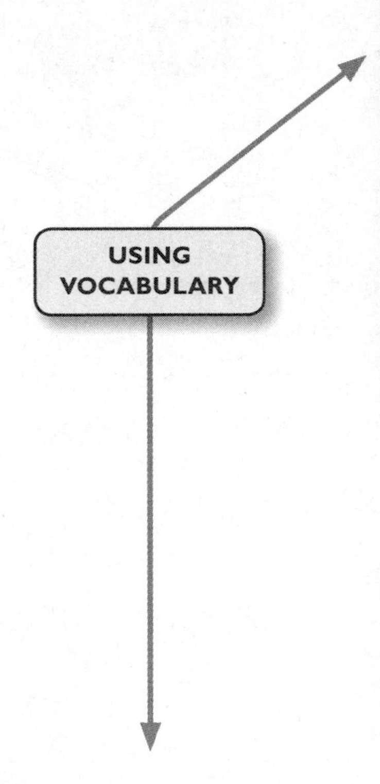

❶ **Apply:** Using Vocabulary—coral polyp (Coral polyps are found in the ocean.)

❷ **Apply:** Using Vocabulary—algae (You might find algae in a fish tank, on the side of a swimming pool, in a pond . . .)

★= New in this unit

2. Now You Try It!

- Read or paraphrase the directions.
- Have students read the word by parts, then read the whole word.
- Have students explain or define the word in their own words. Say something like:

  Look at the word. Say the parts, then read the whole word.
  (col•o•ny, colony)
  Now let's pretend that we're going to explain or define the word *colony* to a friend. [Amanda], what would you say?
  Start with "A *colony* is . . . "
  (A colony is a group of animals that lives together.)
  That's right. A colony is a group of animals that lives together.

- Have students turn to the appropriate page in the glossary and discuss how their definition is the same as or different from the glossary's. Your students may like their definition better.

Note: By defining a word in their own words, students are demonstrating depth of word knowledge. Verbatim responses only demonstrate memorization. Encourage paraphrasing.

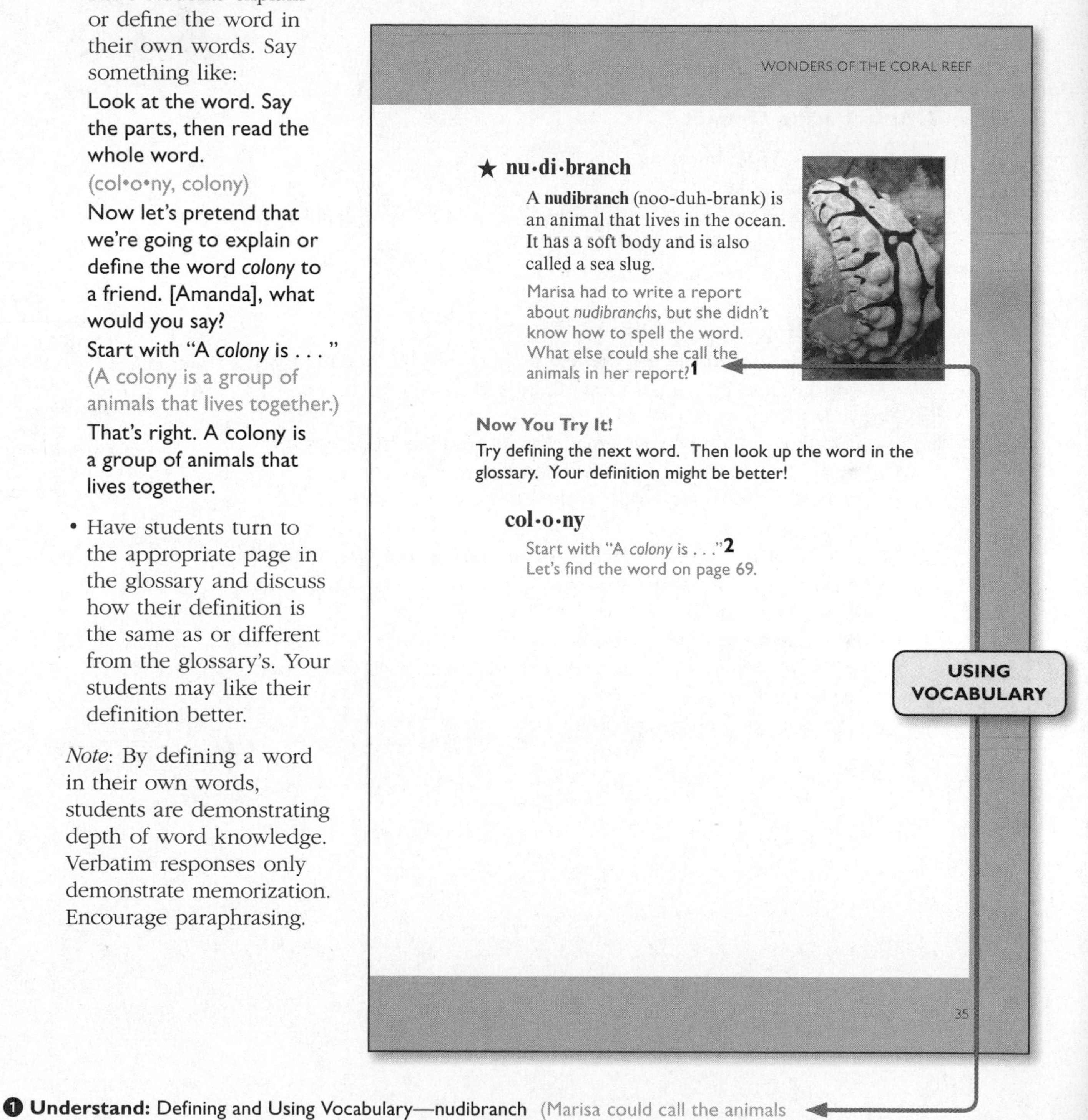

WONDERS OF THE CORAL REEF

★ **nu•di•branch**

A **nudibranch** (noo-duh-brank) is an animal that lives in the ocean. It has a soft body and is also called a sea slug.

Marisa had to write a report about *nudibranchs*, but she didn't know how to spell the word. What else could she call the animals in her report?**1**

Now You Try It!

Try defining the next word. Then look up the word in the glossary. Your definition might be better!

col•o•ny

Start with "A *colony* is . . ."**2**
Let's find the word on page 69.

35

USING VOCABULARY

❶ **Understand:** Defining and Using Vocabulary—nudibranch (Marisa could call the animals in her report sea slugs. Sea slug is another word for nudibranch.)

❷ **Understand:** Defining and Using Vocabulary—colony; Using Glossary (A colony is a group of animals that lives together.)

CHAPTER 1 INSTRUCTIONS

Students read Chapter 1 with the teacher and Chapter 2 on their own.

COMPREHENSION PROCESSES

Understand, Evaluate

PROCEDURES

1. Introducing Chapter 1

Identifying—Title; Inferring

Say something like:

Turn to page 36. What's the title of the first chapter? (Reef Builders)
What do you think the chapter will be about?
(It will be about how the reef was built.)

2. First Reading

- Ask questions and discuss the text as indicated by the gray text.
- Mix group and individual turns, independent of your voice.
  Have students work toward a group accuracy goal of 0–3 errors.
  Quietly keep track of errors made by all students in the group.
- After reading the story, practice any difficult words.
  Repeat, if students have not reached the accuracy goal.

CORRECTING DECODING ERRORS

During story reading, gently correct any error, then have students reread the sentence.

3. Second Reading, Short Passage Practice: Developing Prosody

- Demonstrate expressive, fluent reading of the first paragraph. Read at a rate slightly faster than the students' rate.
- Guide practice with your voice.
- Provide individual turns while others track with their fingers and whisper read.
- Repeat with one paragraph at a time.

WITH THE TEACHER

Reef Builders

Coral polyps are amazing little animals. Across thousands of years, coral polyps have built the Great Barrier Reef.

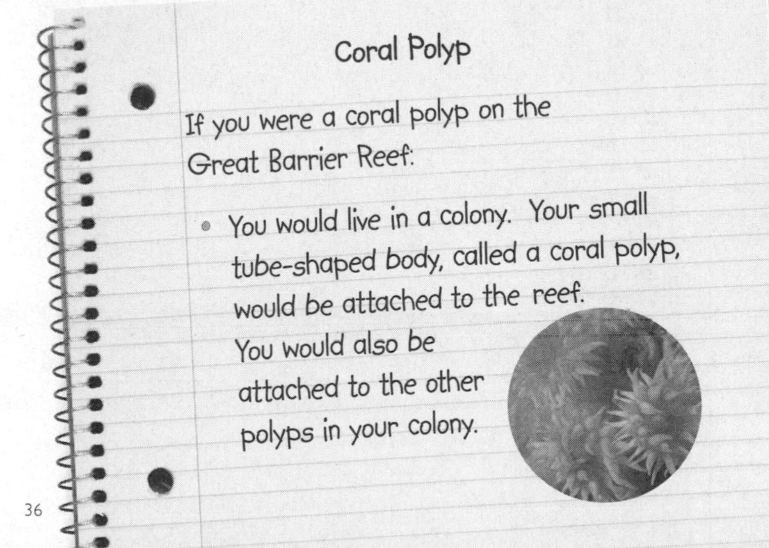

36

COMPREHENSION BUILDING (Reminder)

Encourage students to answer questions with complete sentences. If students have difficulty comprehending, think aloud with them or reread the portion of the story that answers the question. Repeat the question.

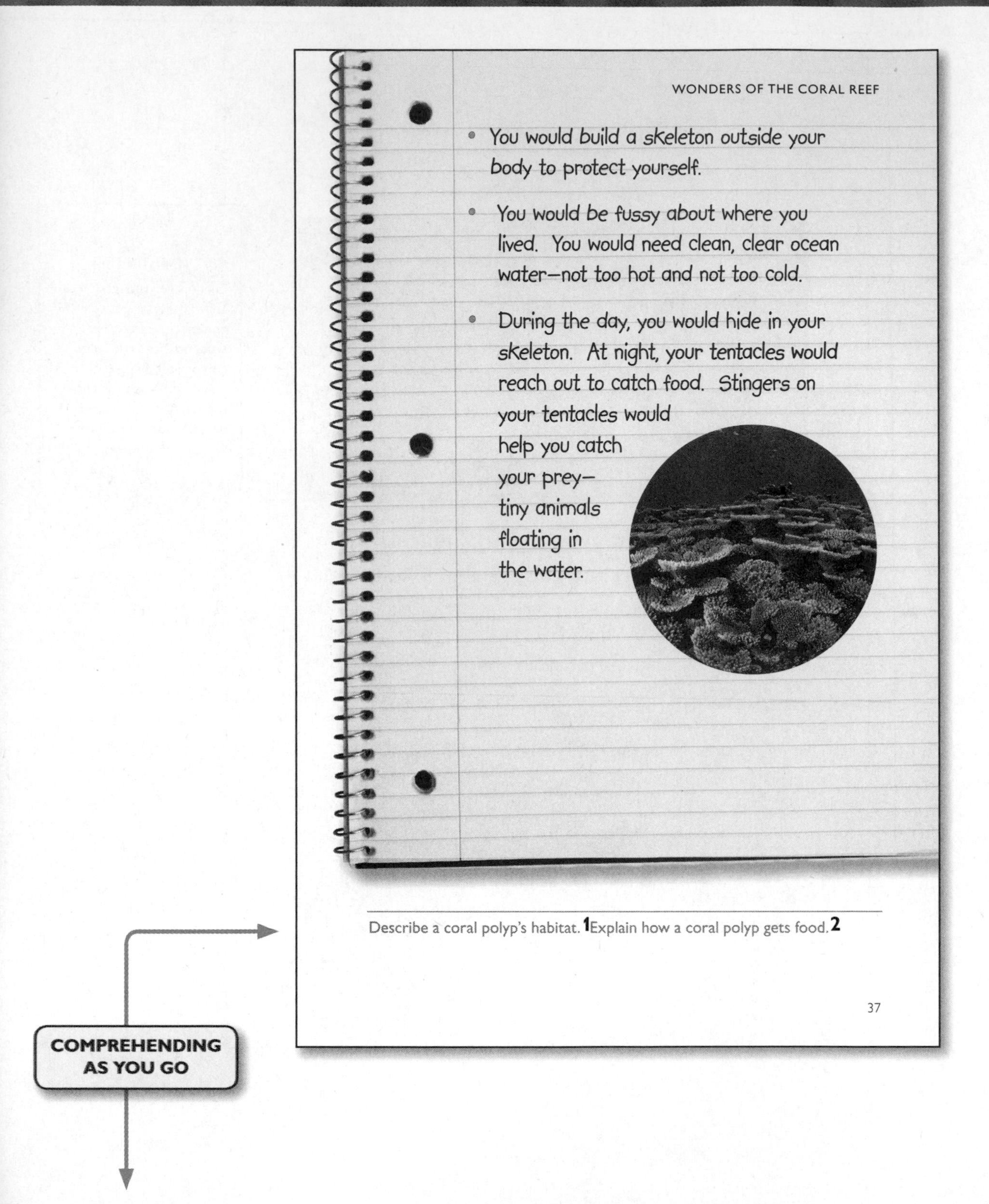

WONDERS OF THE CORAL REEF

- You would build a skeleton outside your body to protect yourself.
- You would be fussy about where you lived. You would need clean, clear ocean water—not too hot and not too cold.
- During the day, you would hide in your skeleton. At night, your tentacles would reach out to catch food. Stingers on your tentacles would help you catch your prey—tiny animals floating in the water.

Describe a coral polyp's habitat. **1** Explain how a coral polyp gets food. **2**

37

COMPREHENDING AS YOU GO

❶ **Understand:** Describing; Summarizing—Facts; Using Vocabulary—habitat, coral polyp, colony, coral reef (A coral polyp lives in a colony. It is attached to other polyps, and it forms a coral reef in the ocean. The ocean water must be clean and not too hot or too cold.)

❷ **Understand:** Explaining; Using Vocabulary—coral polyp (A coral polyp hides in its skeleton. At night, it sticks its tentacles out to catch tiny animals floating by.)

- If you were a coral polyp, tiny algae would grow inside of you—small plant-like things that make energy from the sun. The algae would make you look like you were a wonderful color—red, pink, purple, green, or yellow.
- When you died, you would leave your skeleton behind. New coral polyps would grow on your skeleton. You would still be an important part of the reef.

If you were a little coral polyp, you would be an amazing animal. You would be very important to the blue planet, but you wouldn't know it. Like your relative the jellyfish, you would have no brain!

Think and Talk

FACT

1. What is a coral polyp?

DESCRIPTION

2. Describe a coral polyp.

EXPLANATION

3. Why does a coral polyp build a skeleton outside its body?

EXPLANATION

4. What gives a coral polyp its color?

PERSONAL RESPONSE

5. Would you like to be a coral polyp? Why or why not?

❶ **Understand:** Explaining—Fact; Defining and/or Using Vocabulary—coral polyp, coral reef (A coral polyp is a sea animal with a tube-shaped body. Millions of coral polyps live together to form a coral reef.)

❷ **Understand:** Describing; Using Vocabulary—coral polyp (A coral polyp has a skeleton on the outside of its body. It has tentacles that catch food.)

❸ **Understand:** Explaining; Using Vocabulary—coral polyp, protect (A coral polyp builds its skeleton outside its body to protect itself.)

❹ **Understand:** Explaining; Using Vocabulary—coral polyp; algae (The algae growing inside a coral polyp gives the polyp its color.)

❺ **Evaluate:** Responding; **Understand:** Using Vocabulary—coral polyp (I would not like to be a coral polyp. They are funny looking. It would be boring. I would like to be a coral polyp. It would be nice to be that colorful . . .)

CHAPTER 2 INSTRUCTIONS

Students read without the teacher, independently or with partners.

COMPREHENSION PROCESSES

Remember, Understand

PROCEDURES FOR READING ON YOUR OWN

1. **Getting Ready**
   Have students turn to Chapter 2 on page 40.

2. **Setting a Purpose**

   Identifying—What; Explaining

   Before students begin reading, say something like:
   Read to find out the answers to these questions:
   - What animal can look like a Spanish dancer or a head of lettuce?
   - What can an octopus do to protect itself?
   - What animal has no bones?

> **PREP NOTE**
> **Setting a Purpose**
> Write questions on a chalkboard, white board, or large piece of paper before working with your small group.

3. **Reading on Your Own: Partner or Whisper Reading**
   - Have students take turns reading every other page with a partner or have students whisper read on their own.
   - Continue having students track each word with their fingers.

4. **Comprehension and Skill Work**
   For students on a 6-Day Plan, tell them they will do Comprehension and Skill Activities 5a and 5b after they read on their own. Guide practice, as needed. For teacher directions, see pages 72 and 73. (For 8- to 11-Day Plans, see the Lesson Planner, page 9.)

5. **Homework 3: Repeated Reading**

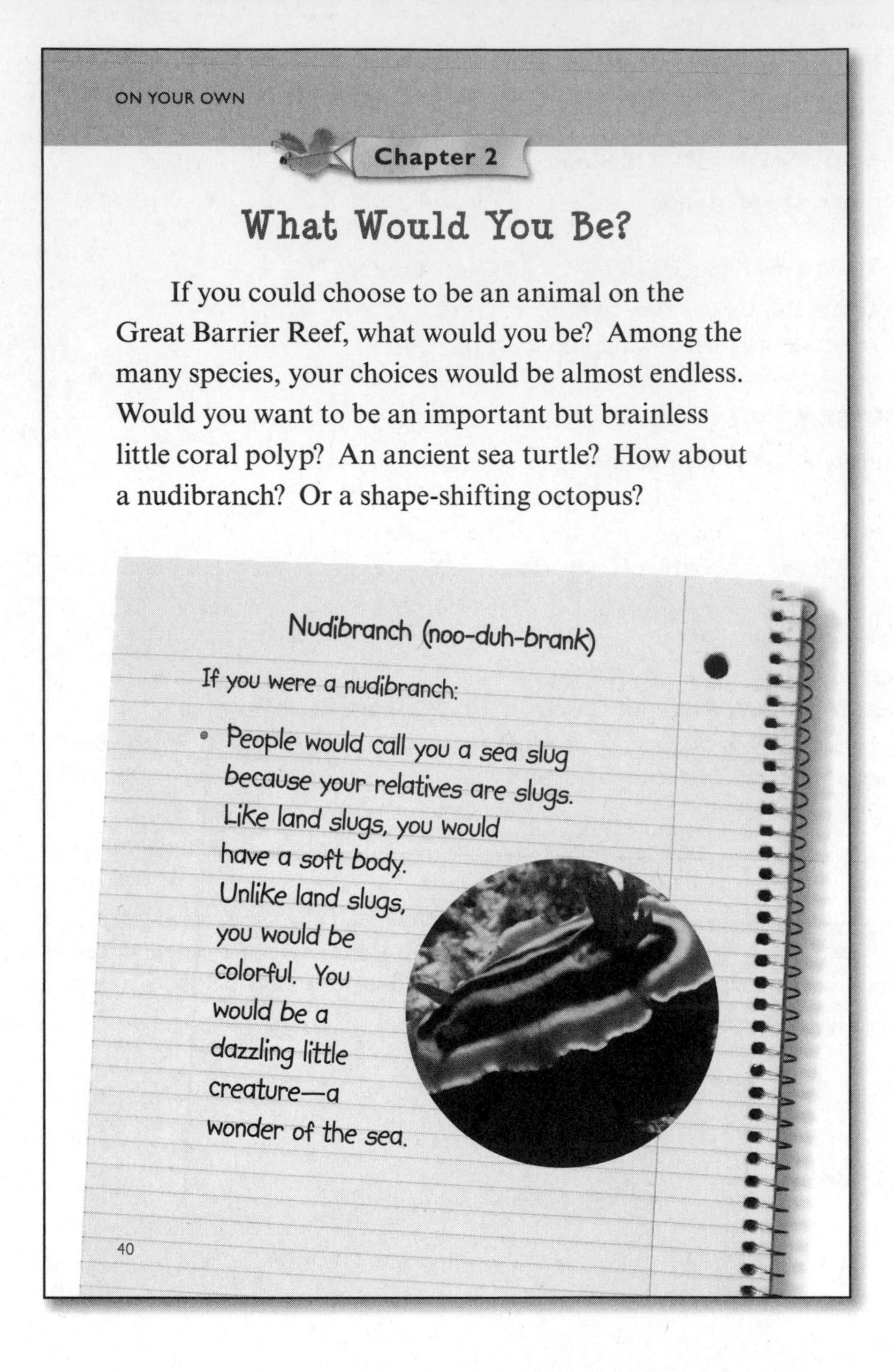

ON YOUR OWN

Chapter 2

What Would You Be?

If you could choose to be an animal on the Great Barrier Reef, what would you be? Among the many species, your choices would be almost endless. Would you want to be an important but brainless little coral polyp? An ancient sea turtle? How about a nudibranch? Or a shape-shifting octopus?

Nudibranch (noo-duh-brank)

If you were a nudibranch:

- People would call you a sea slug because your relatives are slugs. Like land slugs, you would have a soft body. Unlike land slugs, you would be colorful. You would be a dazzling little creature—a wonder of the sea.

40

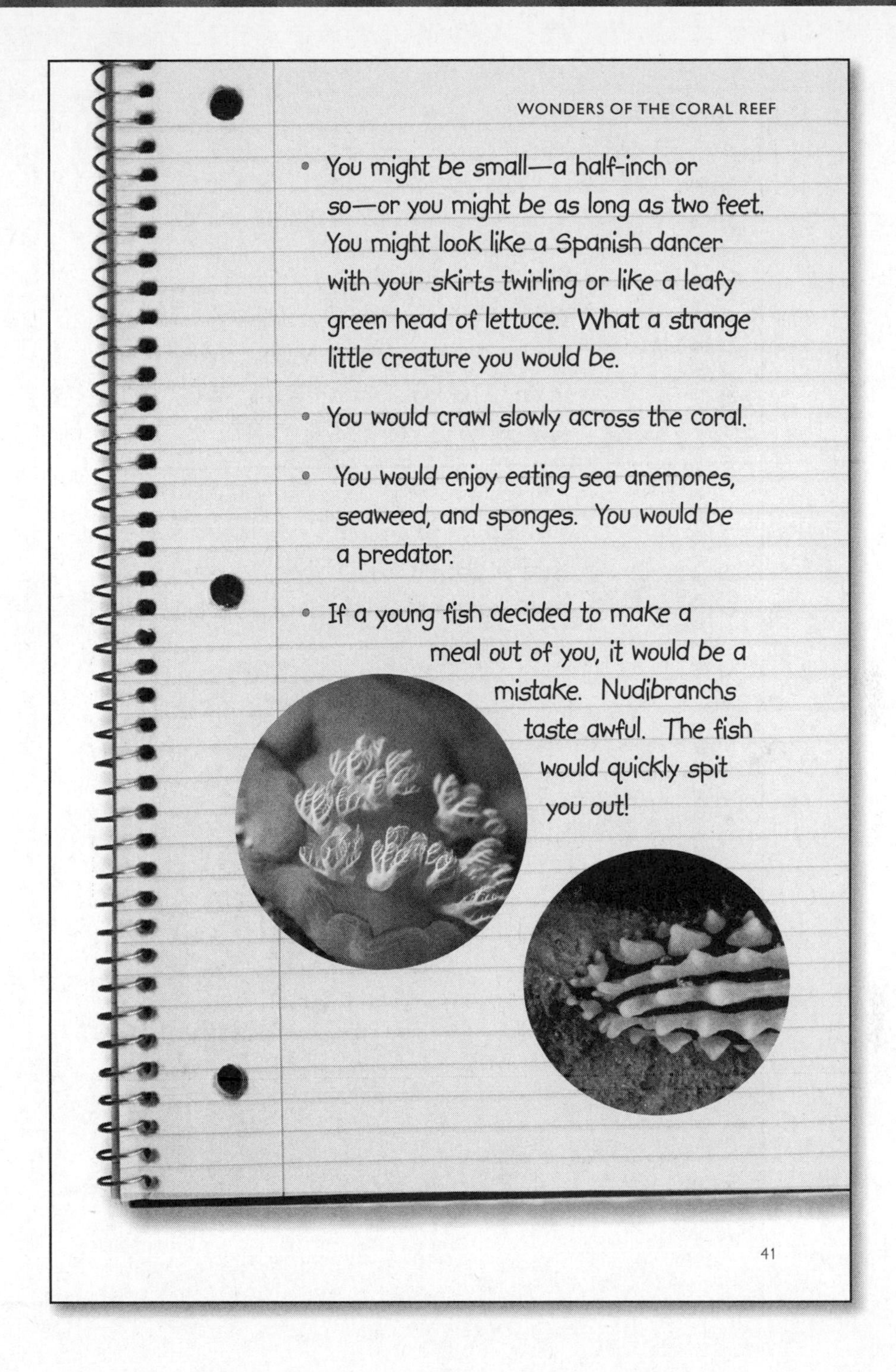
WONDERS OF THE CORAL REEF

- You might be small—a half-inch or so—or you might be as long as two feet. You might look like a Spanish dancer with your skirts twirling or like a leafy green head of lettuce. What a strange little creature you would be.
- You would crawl slowly across the coral.
- You would enjoy eating sea anemones, seaweed, and sponges. You would be a predator.
- If a young fish decided to make a meal out of you, it would be a mistake. Nudibranchs taste awful. The fish would quickly spit you out!

41

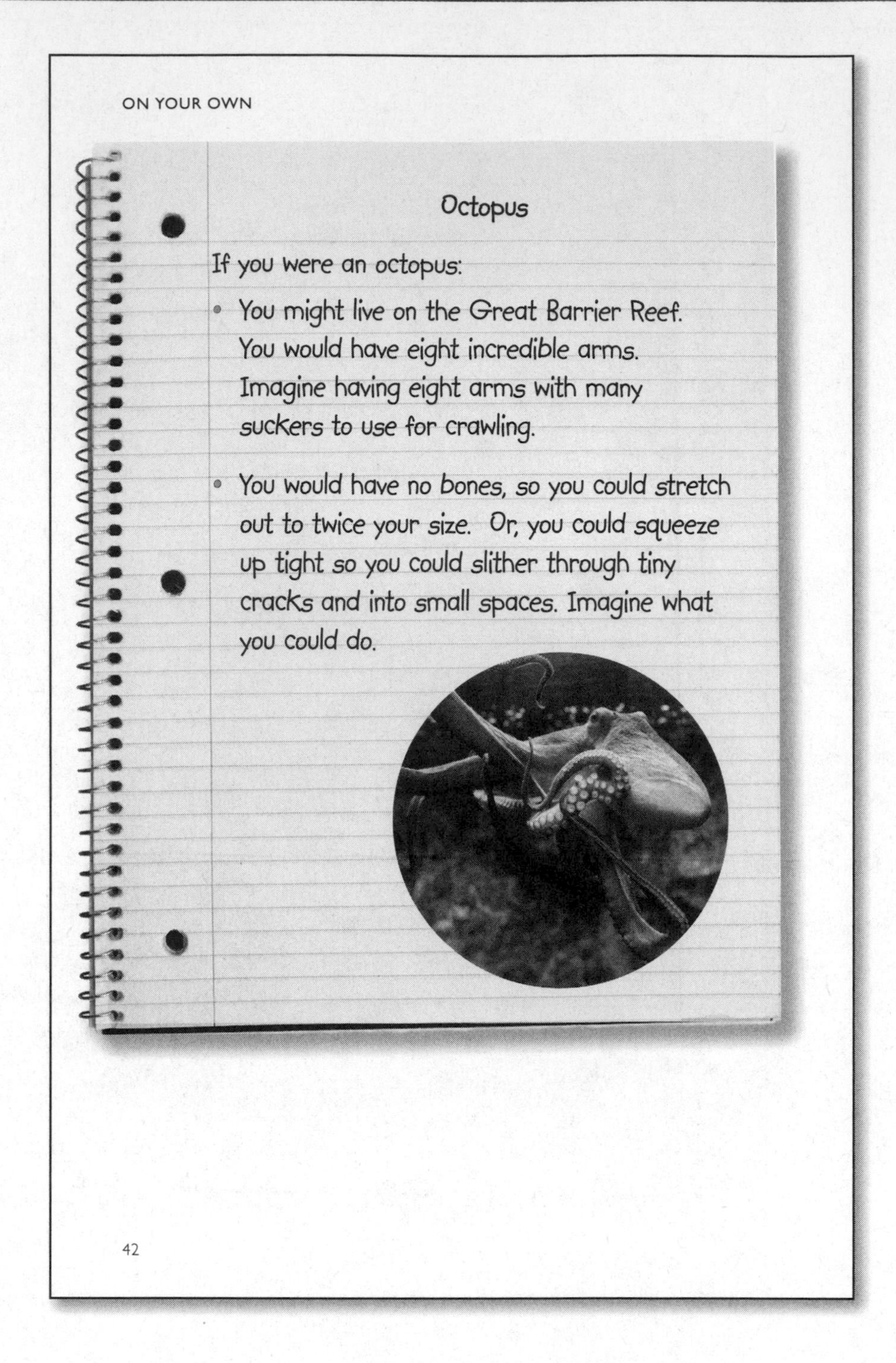

ON YOUR OWN

Octopus

If you were an octopus:

- You might live on the Great Barrier Reef. You would have eight incredible arms. Imagine having eight arms with many suckers to use for crawling.
- You would have no bones, so you could stretch out to twice your size. Or, you could squeeze up tight so you could slither through tiny cracks and into small spaces. Imagine what you could do.

42

- If a diver visited your home, you would play hide-and-seek. You would be hard to spot. You would change your color. You would be a master of disguise. You would make your skin look bumpy like the coral or smooth like a sponge.
- If someone got too close, you might even squirt a cloud of black ink and quickly swim away!

If you could choose to be an animal on the Great Barrier Reef, what would you be?

WRITTEN RETELL

COMPREHENSION PROCESSES

Understand

WRITING TRAITS

Ideas and Content
Organization—Sequencing
Word Choice
Conventions—Complete Sentence, Capital, Period
Presentation

Explaining—Setting, Main Character
Describing—Character Traits (Characterization)

Summarizing, Sequencing
Sentence Writing

Explaining—Beginning, Initiating Event

Summarizing—Middle, Action

Wonders of the Coral Reef

Unit 18 Activity 5a
Use after Exercise 3 and Chapters 1 and 2

Name ____________

Written Retell
Miss Tam at the Great Barrier Reef

◆ **INTRODUCTION • Setting/Main Character:** Tell where the story takes place and who the main character is. Write at least two sentences.

This story is about the retired librarian Miss Tam and her trip to the Great Barrier Reef. Miss Tam loves to travel all over the world.

● **BEGINNING • Initiating Event:** Write what happened at the beginning of the story.

Miss Tam wanted to go on a dive at the Great Barrier Reef. She wanted to see pufferfish and octopuses.

■ **MIDDLE • Action:** Write what Miss Tam did at the Great Barrier Reef.

First, Miss Tam went on a boat to the Great Barrier Reef.

Next, she had to squeeze into her wetsuit. Then she had to put on more equipment and do a safety check.

continued

65

PROCEDURES

Use an overhead BLM copy of the story map to demonstrate and guide how to create a written retell.

Written Retell: Paragraph Writing—Basic Instructions

- Guide students, only as needed, as they construct an introductory paragraph using the information from their story map. You may wish to brainstorm phrases that describe the main character before they start.
- Repeat for the beginning and middle of the story, using the information from the story map. Remind students to start each sentence with a capital and end with a period.

WRITTEN RETELL *(continued)*

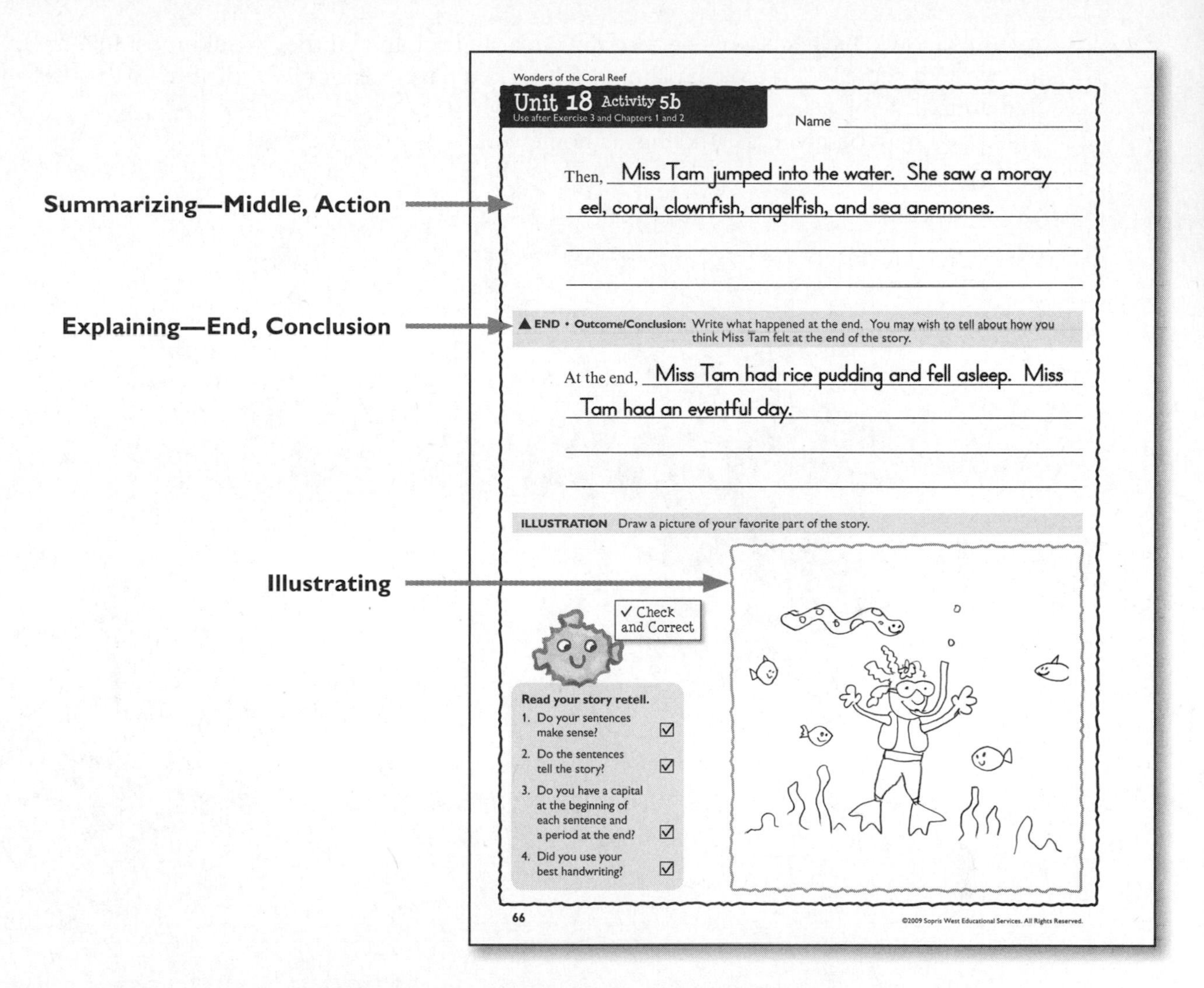

Wonders of the Coral Reef

Unit 18 Activity 5b
Use after Exercise 3 and Chapters 1 and 2

Name ______________________

Then, Miss Tam jumped into the water. She saw a moray eel, coral, clownfish, angelfish, and sea anemones.

▲ **END • Outcome/Conclusion:** Write what happened at the end. You may wish to tell about how you think Miss Tam felt at the end of the story.

At the end, Miss Tam had rice pudding and fell asleep. Miss Tam had an eventful day.

ILLUSTRATION Draw a picture of your favorite part of the story.

✓ Check and Correct

Read your story retell.

1. Do your sentences make sense? ☑
2. Do the sentences tell the story? ☑
3. Do you have a capital at the beginning of each sentence and a period at the end? ☑
4. Did you use your best handwriting? ☑

66

Written Retell: Paragraph Writing—Basic Instructions *(continued)*

- Guide students as they finish summarizing the middle, then have them construct an ending paragraph based on information in the story map.
- Have students check and correct their work, then illustrate their favorite part of the story.

JUST FOR FUN • IF I WERE . . .

PROCEDURES

As time allows, have students choose the Great Barrier animal they would most like to be and write a sentence or two explaining why. Then have them draw a picture of themselves as that animal.

This page may be given to students as homework.

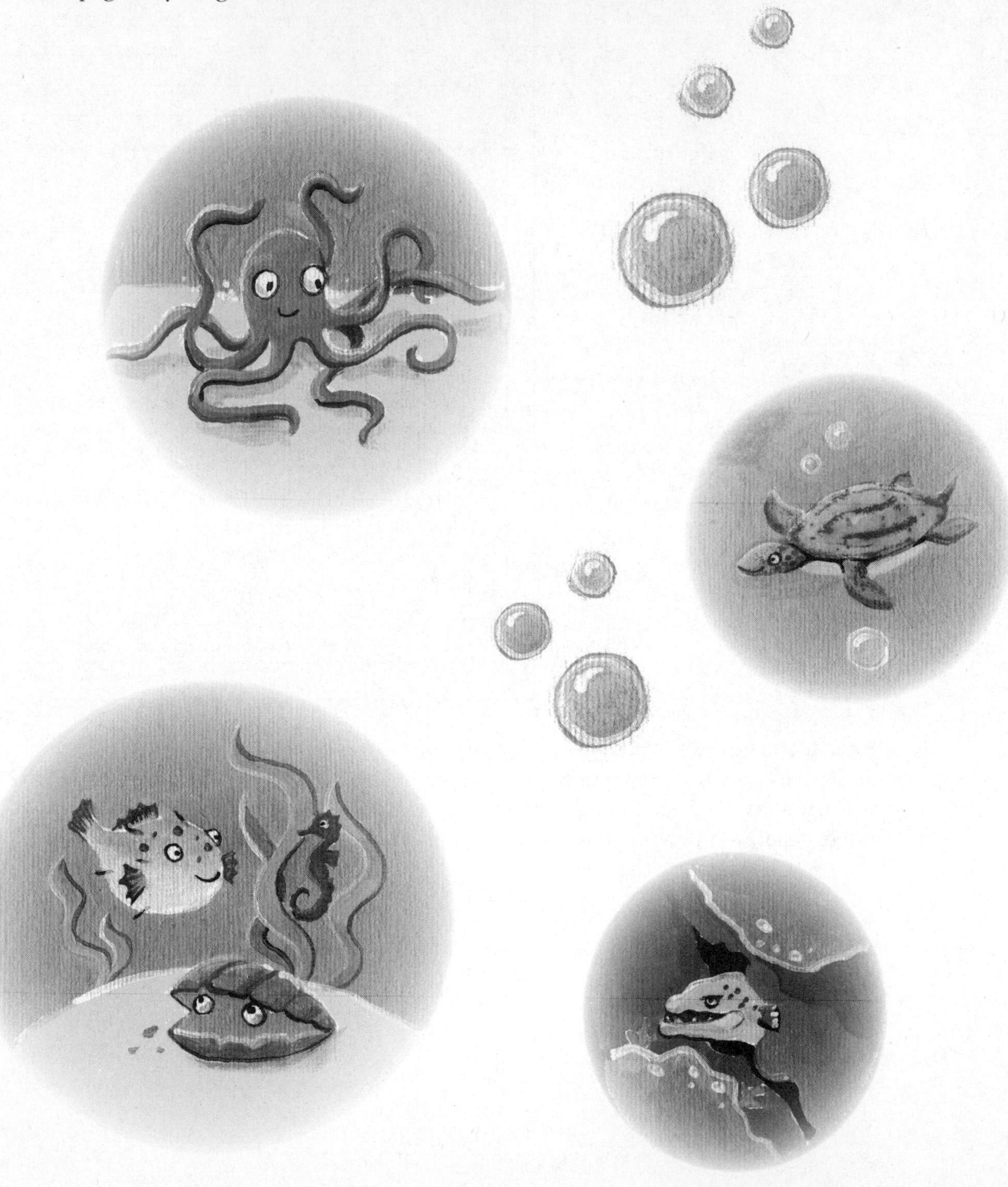

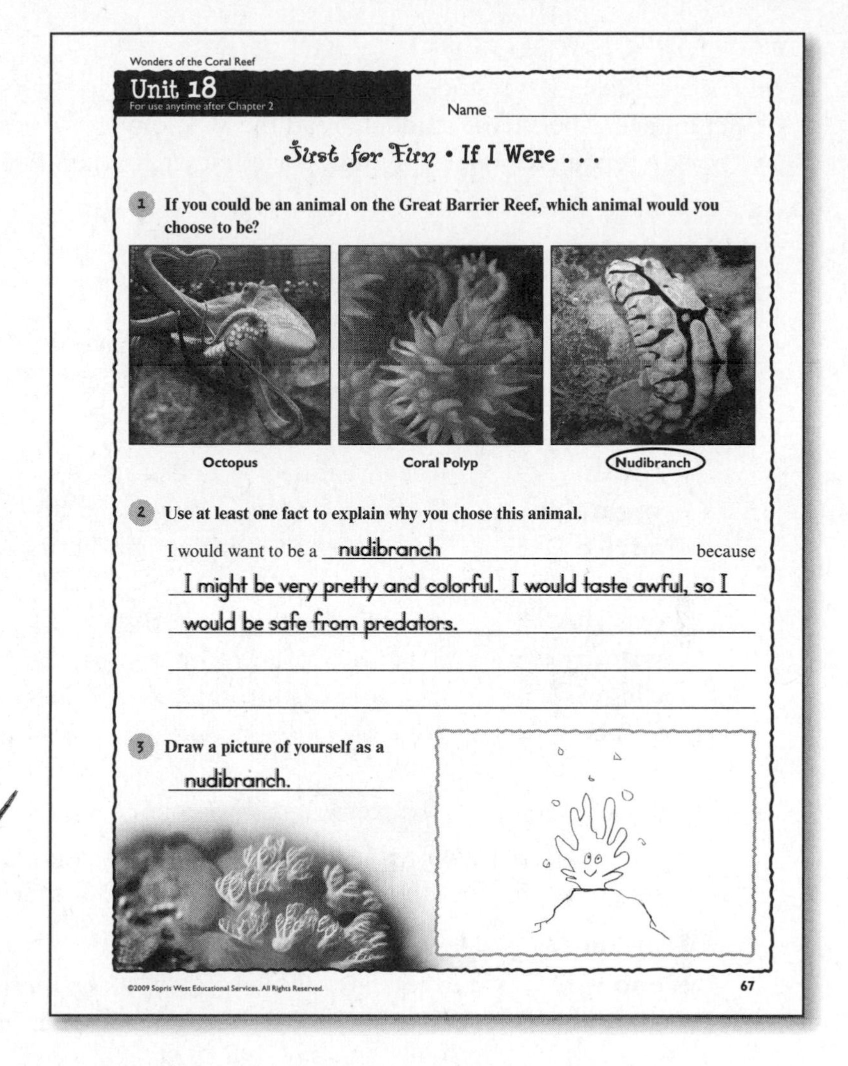
Wonders of the Coral Reef

Unit 18
For use anytime after Chapter 2

Name ______________________

Just for Fun • If I Were . . .

1 **If you could be an animal on the Great Barrier Reef, which animal would you choose to be?**

Octopus | Coral Polyp | Nudibranch

2 **Use at least one fact to explain why you chose this animal.**

I would want to be a nudibranch because I might be very pretty and colorful. I would taste awful, so I would be safe from predators.

3 **Draw a picture of yourself as a** nudibranch.

67

HOW TO USE "JUST FOR FUN" ACTIVITIES

Note: This activity is optional and is *just for fun.* Use the activity:

- as a cushion activity
- for homework
- just for fun

❶ SOUND REVIEW

Have students read the sounds and key word phrases. Work for accuracy, then fluency.

❷ ACCURACY AND FLUENCY BUILDING

- For each task, have students say any underlined part, then read the word.
- Set a pace. Then have students read the whole words in each task and column.
- Provide repeated practice, building accuracy first, then fluency.

B1. Bossy E

Have students identify the underlined sound and then read the word.

C1. Multisyllabic Words

- For the list of words divided by syllables, have students read each syllable, then the whole word. Use the word in a sentence, as appropriate.
- For the list of whole words, build accuracy and then fluency.

coral The Great Barrier Reef is made of . . . *coral.*
vegetable A carrot is a long, orange-colored . . . *vegetable.*
advice The young girl didn't know what to do, so she went to her mom for . . . *advice.*
octopus An animal with eight arms is an . . . *octopus.*
wilderness Blake and his uncle went camping in the . . . *wilderness.*
disguise The girls went to the costume party and wore a great . . . *disguise.*
safety A police officer came to our class to teach a lesson about bicycle . . . *safety.*

D1. Tricky Words

- For each Tricky Word, have students use the sounds and word parts they know to silently sound out the word. Use the word in a sentence to help with pronunciation.

unique His shirt was one of a kind. It was . . . *unique.*
enough She couldn't lift the heavy book because she wasn't strong . . . *enough.*
stomach Food that you chew and swallow goes into your . . . *stomach.*
toward Jack didn't see the car until he turned . . . *toward* . . . it.

- Have students go back and read the whole words in the column.

❸ WORD ENDINGS

Have students read any underlined word, then the word with an ending.
Note: Tell students you drop the e when you add *-ing* to "giggle" and "change."

❹ MORPHOGRAPHS AND AFFIXES

- Have students read "-less equals without" and the accompanying word and sentence. Then have students explain the sentence.
- For Rows B and C, have students read the underlined part, then the word.
- Repeat practice with whole words, mixing group and individual turns. Build accuracy, then fluency.

❺ GENERALIZATION: READING NEW WORDS IN PARAGRAPHS

- Have students read the paragraph silently, then out loud. Tell students to use the sounds and word parts they know to read any difficult words.
- Repeat practice, as needed.

Unit 18 Exercise 4

Use before Chapters 1 and 2

1. SOUND REVIEW Have students review sounds for accuracy, then for fluency.

A	au as in astronaut	ow as in snow	-y as in fly	ea as in bread	aw as in paw
B	ew	-dge	oy	oi	oa

2. ACCURACY/FLUENCY BUILDING For each column, have students say any underlined part, then read each word. Next, have them read the column.

A1 Mixed Practice	B1 Bossy E	C1 Multisyllabic Words		D1 Tricky Words
blue	wise	cor•al	coral	unique
peace	Pete	vege•ta•ble	vegetable	enough
shell	amazed	ad•vice	advice	stomach
moray	**B2** Compound Words	oc•to•pus	octopus	toward
explored	itself	wil•der•ness	wilderness	
grumpy	pufferfish	dis•guise	disguise	
grown	Grandfather	safe•ty	safety	
growths				

3. WORD ENDINGS Have students read any underlined word, then the word with an ending.

A	blended	squeezed	swooshed	squished
B	giggle	giggling	change	changing

4. MORPHOGRAPHS AND AFFIXES Have students practice reading "-less = without" and the related word and sentence. For Rows B and C, have students read the underlined part, then the word.

A	-less = without	harmless = without harm	The sea creature was harmless.	
B	exclaimed	barely	commotion	dangerous
C	occasion	rudeness	advisor	happiness

5. GENERALIZATION Have students read the paragraph silently, then out loud. (New words: slender, seahorse, spiny lobster)

The Great Barrier Reef is one of the seven wonders of the natural world. It is filled with incredible, interesting sea creatures, such as the slender and graceful seahorse, the spiny lobster, and the giant clam. Would you like to visit the Great Barrier Reef someday?

MIX IT UP (Reminder)

Response forms can be varied. Have students say the sounds using different rhythms. Have students use big voices, small voices, and deep voices. Pass the cards to students. Then have them find and return a sound. Be creative, but maintain a high rate of group responses.

COMPREHENSION PROCESSES

Remember, Understand, Apply

PROCEDURES

1. Reviewing Chapter 2 (Wonders of the Coral Reef)

Summarizing; Identifying—What; Using Vocabulary—protect

Have students turn to page 40. Quickly discuss the questions from Chapter 2, Setting a Purpose. Say something like:

Yesterday, you read Chapter 2 on your own. Let's see what you found out. What animal can look like a Spanish dancer or a head of lettuce? (a nudibranch)

What can an octopus do to protect itself? (An octopus can protect itself by changing its color and shape and by squirting ink.)

What animal has no bones? (an octopus)

2. Introducing the Story

Using Table of Contents; Identifying—Title, Where; Classifying—Genre; Inferring; Locating Information; Priming Background Knowledge

Have students find the Table of Contents for Unit 18.

What's the title of your new story? (Pete the Pufferfish)

What kind of story is "Pete the Pufferfish"? (fiction)

Where do you think Pete lives? (Pete lives near a reef in the ocean.)

Yes, you already know a lot about the setting.

What kind of fish is Pete? (Pete is a pufferfish.)

It seems like we read something about a pufferfish before.

Look at page 2 of the Table of Contents. Do you remember what story the pufferfish was in? (I think it was in the story about food chains.)

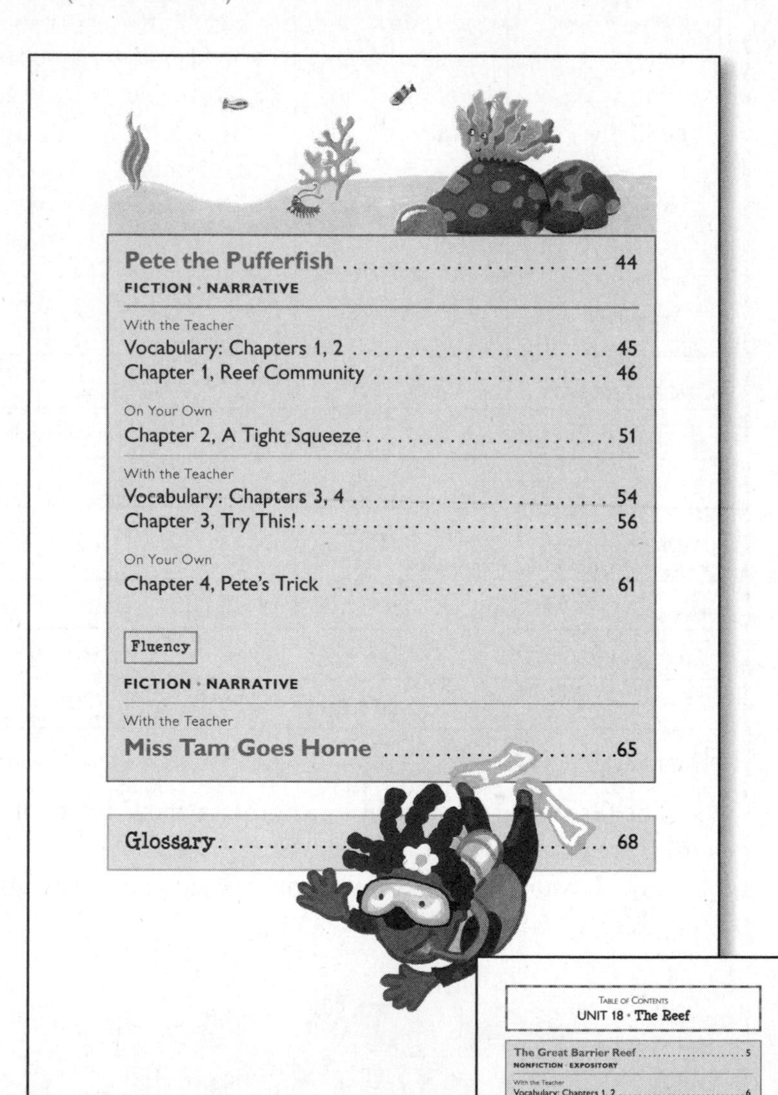

TABLE OF CONTENTS
UNIT 18 • The Reef

2

Find the chapter that was about food chains. What page should we turn to first? (page 14)

Great. Turn to page 14. That's where Chapter 2 of "The Great Barrier Reef" begins.

Now find the part about the pufferfish.

What did you learn about the pufferfish? (It can puff itself up. It's an omnivore . . .)

3. Introducing the Title Page

Identifying—Authors

Have students identify the authors and discuss the gray text question. Say something like:

There's Pete, the little pufferfish. As you read, remember what you know about pufferfish. You may be able to predict what will happen.

Who are the authors?
(Jessica Sprick and Marilyn Sprick)

❶ **Understand:** Viewing, Describing (I see a pufferfish, coral, other little fish, a shrimp . . .)

COMPREHENSION PROCESSES

Understand, Apply

PROCEDURES

1. Introducing Vocabulary

★disguise ★advisor, coral reef

- For each vocabulary word, have students read the word by parts, then read the whole word.
- Read the student-friendly explanations to students as they follow with their fingers. Then have students use the vocabulary word by following the gray text.
- Review and discuss the photos and illustrations.

2. Now You Try It!

- Read or paraphrase the directions.
- Then have students read the word by parts and then read the whole word.
- Have students explain or define the word in their own words.
- Have students turn to the appropriate page in the glossary and discuss how their definition is the same as or different from the glossary's. Your students may like their definition better.

Note: By defining a word in their own words, students are demonstrating depth of word knowledge. Verbatim responses only demonstrate memorization. Encourage paraphrasing.

★= New in this unit

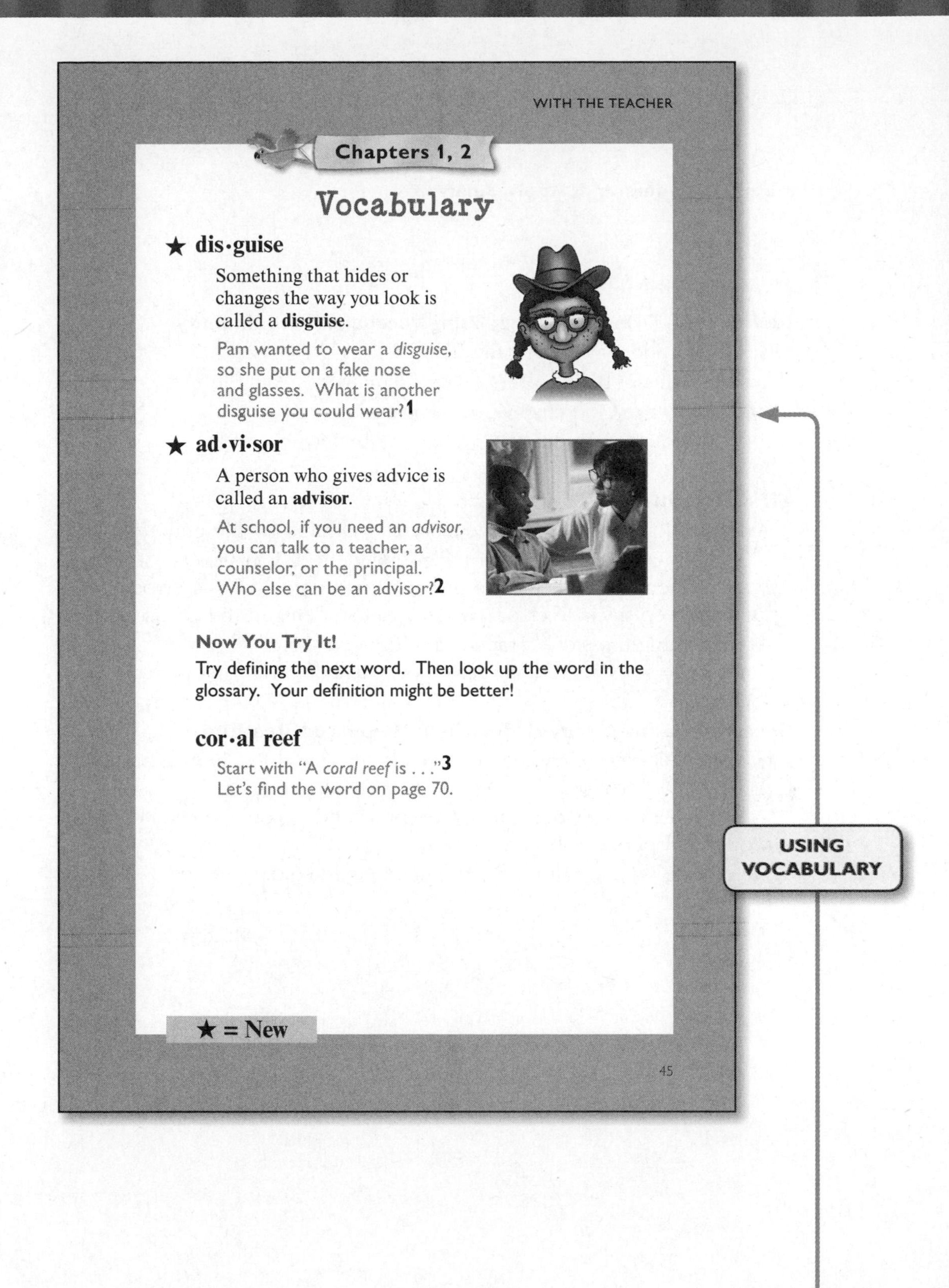

WITH THE TEACHER

Chapters 1, 2

Vocabulary

★ **dis·guise**

Something that hides or changes the way you look is called a **disguise**.

Pam wanted to wear a *disguise*, so she put on a fake nose and glasses. What is another disguise you could wear? **1**

★ **ad·vi·sor**

A person who gives advice is called an **advisor**.

At school, if you need an *advisor*, you can talk to a teacher, a counselor, or the principal. Who else can be an advisor? **2**

Now You Try It!

Try defining the next word. Then look up the word in the glossary. Your definition might be better!

cor·al reef

Start with "A *coral reef* is . . ." **3**
Let's find the word on page 70.

★ = New

45

❶ **Apply:** Using Vocabulary—disguise (You could wear a wig and a fake mustache as a disguise, or a mask . . .)

❷ **Apply:** Using Vocabulary—advisor (A parent can be an advisor. A scout leader can be an advisor. A friend . . .)

❸ **Understand:** Defining and Using Vocabulary—coral reef, habitat, coral polyp; Using Glossary (A coral reef is an underwater habitat built by small animals called coral polyps.)

CHAPTER 1 INSTRUCTIONS

Students read Chapter 1 with the teacher and Chapter 2 on their own.

COMPREHENSION PROCESSES

Remember, Understand, Apply, Analyze

PROCEDURES

1. Introducing Chapter 1

Identifying—Title; Predicting; Using Vocabulary—community

Discuss the title. Say something like:

What's the title of this chapter? (Reef Community)

What do you think this chapter will be about?

(It will be about a community of sea animals that live together.)

2. First Reading

- Ask questions and discuss the story as indicated by the gray text.
- Mix group and individual turns, independent of your voice.
  Have students work toward a group accuracy goal of 0–4 errors.
  Quietly keep track of errors made by all students in the group.
- After reading the story, practice any difficult words.
  Reread the story if students have not reached the accuracy goal.

3. Second Reading, Timed Readings: Repeated Reading

- As time allows, have students do Timed Readings while others follow along.
- Time individuals for 30 seconds and encourage each child to work for a personal best.
- Determine words correct per minute. Record student scores.

WITH THE TEACHER

Chapter 1

Reef Community

Long, long ago on a busy ocean reef, there lived a little spotted pufferfish named Pete. Pete hatched from an egg on the ocean floor. Then he drifted in the big open ocean. Pete loved the peace and quiet of his ocean home.

But Pete, like other pufferfish, couldn't stay in the open ocean. It was far too dangerous. When he was big enough, he decided to make his way to the safety of the Great Barrier Reef.

Why did Pete need to make his way to the Great Barrier Reef?1

46

COMPREHENDING AS YOU GO

1 **Understand:** Explaining; Using Vocabulary—dangerous (It was too dangerous to stay in the open ocean.)

Once at the big reef, Pete was amazed by all the commotion. Strange and wonderful animals zipped and swooshed in the water around him. Purple, blue, green, yellow . . . spotted, striped, and spiny fish zoomed past. Animals squeezed through cracks in the rocks and darted in and out of the coral. Then Pete saw a very strange sight. "That lettuce is walking!" he exclaimed.

Describe Pete's new home. **1**

COMPREHENDING AS YOU GO

❶ **Understand:** Describing—Setting; Using Vocabulary—coral (The reef is busy with lots of animals. The animals are very colorful, and some are strange looking. There's a lot of colorful coral . . .)

WITH THE TEACHER

Just then Pete heard a giggle. The lettuce was giggling! "Ha! Fooled you," said the walking vegetable. "I'm Sasha the Sea Slug."

Pete laughed. Sasha had green leafy-looking growths on her body that looked like lettuce. Sasha had grown a disguise. The reef was much more interesting than Pete had ever dreamed.

Pete explored the wonders of the reef. He made friends. Calm Mother Octopus and wise Grandfather Sea Turtle became his advisors. The reef was an incredible community.

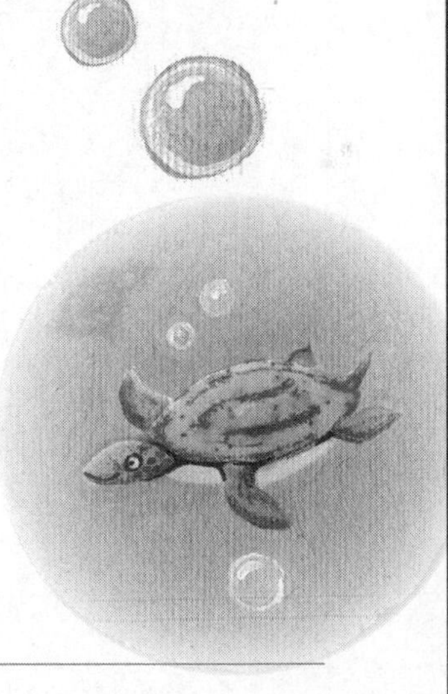

Why do you think Sasha looked like lettuce? 1
Who were Pete's advisors? 2 What do advisors do? 3

48

COMPREHENDING AS YOU GO

❶ **Analyze:** Drawing Conclusions; **Apply:** Using Vocabulary—disguise, protect, predator (Sasha looked like lettuce because that was her disguise. She needed a disguise to protect herself from predators.)

❷ **Remember:** Identifying—Who; Using Vocabulary—advisor (Mother Octopus and Grandfather Sea Turtle were Pete's advisors.)

❸ **Understand:** Defining and/or Using Vocabulary—advisor, advice (Advisors give advice to others.)

Pete was amazed at how different all of the animals were. They all had special ways to survive in the ocean wilderness. The tiny little seahorse could change colors, the giant clam had a big thick shell, and the grumpy moray eel blended into the cracks of the rocks.

As Pete settled into his new life on the Great Barrier Reef, he decided to learn how to protect himself.

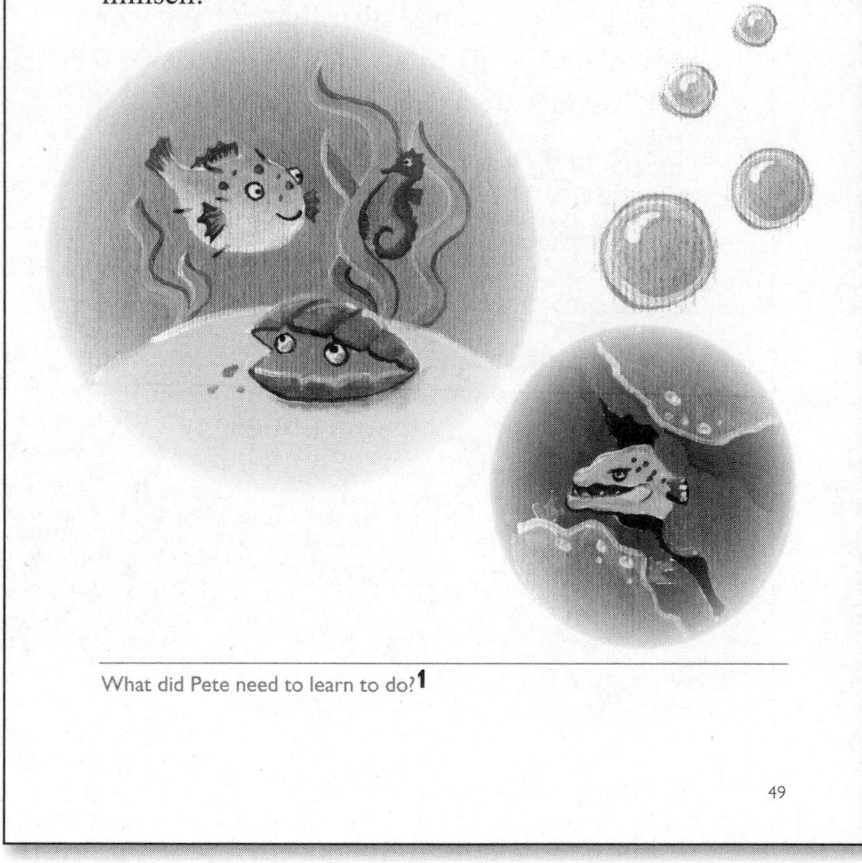

What did Pete need to learn to do?[1]

COMPREHENDING AS YOU GO

1 Understand: Identifying—Goal; Using Vocabulary—protect (Pete needed to learn how to protect himself.)

WITH THE TEACHER

SETTING

1. Where does the story take place?

MAIN CHARACTER, GOAL

2. Who is the main character, and what does he want?

DESCRIPTION

3. Describe Pete's friends.

PREDICTION

4. How do you think Mother Octopus and Grandfather Sea Turtle will help Pete?

50

❶ **Remember:** Identifying—Setting (The story takes place at the Great Barrier Reef.)

❷ **Remember:** Identifying—Main Character; **Understand:** Explaining—Goal; Using Vocabulary—protect (Pete the Pufferfish is the main character, and his goal is to find a way to protect himself.)

❸ **Understand:** Describing (Sasha the Sea Slug is friendly and giggly. Mother Octopus is calm, and Grandfather Sea Turtle is wise.)

❹ **Apply:** Predicting; Using Vocabulary—advisor, advice, protect (They are his advisors. They will tell him how to protect himself. They will give him advice.)

CHAPTER 2 INSTRUCTIONS

Students read without the teacher, independently or with partners.

COMPREHENSION PROCESSES

Understand

PROCEDURES FOR READING ON YOUR OWN

1. Getting Ready

Have students turn to Chapter 2 on page 51.

2. Setting a Purpose

Explaining; Using Vocabulary—advice, protect; Inferring

Before students begin reading, say something like:

As you read the next pages, try to answer these questions:

- What was Mother Octopus's advice?
- Why was it hard for Pete to protect himself like Mother Octopus?

> **PREP NOTE**
> **Setting a Purpose**
> Write questions on a chalkboard, white board, or large piece of paper before working with your small group.

3. Reading on Your Own: Partner or Whisper Reading

- Have students take turns reading every other page with a partner or have students whisper read on their own.
- Continue having students track each word with their fingers.
- Have students ask themselves or their partners the gray text questions.

4. Comprehension and Skill Work

For students on a 6-Day Plan, tell them they will do Comprehension and Skill Activities 6 and 7 after they read on their own. Guide practice, as needed. For teacher directions, see pages 92 and 93. (For 8- to 11-Day Plans, see the Lesson Planner, page 9.)

5. Homework 4: Repeated Reading

ON YOUR OWN

A Tight Squeeze

Pete swam over to see Mother Octopus and Grandfather Sea Turtle. He hoped they would have good advice. Pete said, "Mother Octopus and Grandfather Sea Turtle, there are many different animals on this reef, and it seems that every animal has a different way to protect itself. But I don't know how to stay safe from the fish that want to eat me. Can you help me?"

Mother Octopus crossed two of her long slender arms as she thought about Pete's question. Finally, she said, "I can teach you how to stay safe from hungry animals. Follow me."

Mother Octopus swam toward a small crack in the rocks below. She looked at Pete and said, "When danger is near, you must hide!" Then Mother Octopus said, "Think about changing your shape to fit where you want to go. Suck in your stomach and squeeze. Watch."

How is Mother Octopus trying to help Pete?[1] What is her advice?[2]

51

COMPREHENDING AS YOU GO

❶ **Understand:** Explaining; Using Vocabulary—advice, protect (She is giving him advice about how to hide and protect himself.)

❷ **Understand:** Explaining; Using Vocabulary—advice (She tells him to hide when danger is near.)

Mother Octopus disappeared into the tiny crack. Pete looked at Grandfather Sea Turtle. The ancient turtle shrugged his flippers. He wasn't so sure Pete could squeeze into the tiny crack. Pete had a bit of a round belly. Mother Octopus called from inside the crack, "Come on, Pete! You can do it!"

Pete thought and thought about changing his shape. His face turned blue. He sucked in his stomach so hard he could barely breathe. Then Pete squished himself as far as he could into the crack. "I DID IT! Mother Octopus, I did it!" Pete cried. But as soon as Pete spoke, his little stomach popped out. He was stuck.

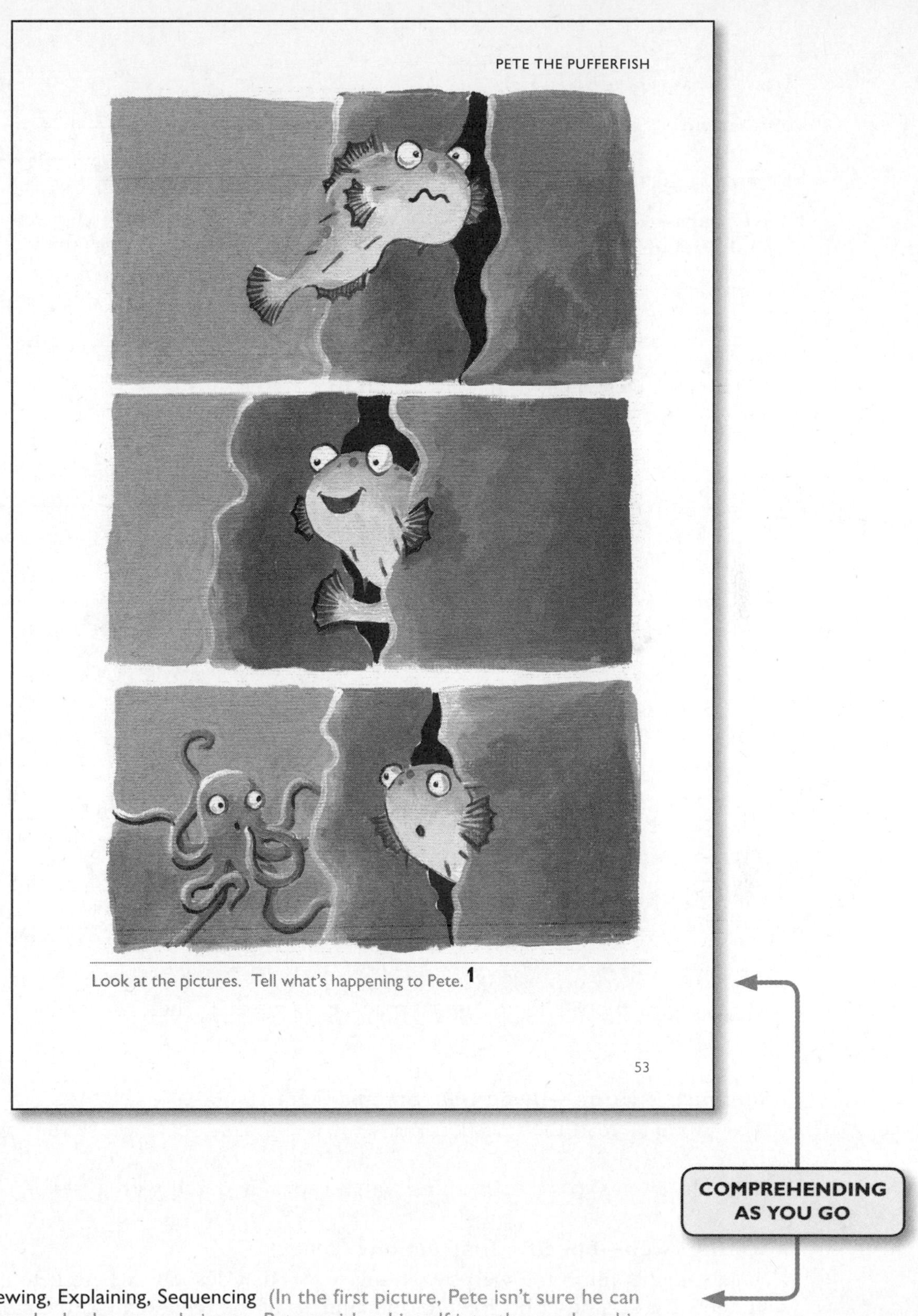

COMPREHENDING AS YOU GO

❶ **Understand:** Viewing, Explaining, Sequencing (In the first picture, Pete isn't sure he can squeeze into the crack. In the second picture, Pete squishes himself into the crack and is very happy about it. In the last picture, his stomach pops out, and he gets stuck.)

SETTING WEB

COMPREHENSION PROCESSES

Understand

WRITING TRAITS

Conventions—Complete Sentence, Capital, Period

Explaining—Setting

Locating Information; Using Graphic Organizer; Describing—Setting
Using Vocabulary—coral reef, Australia

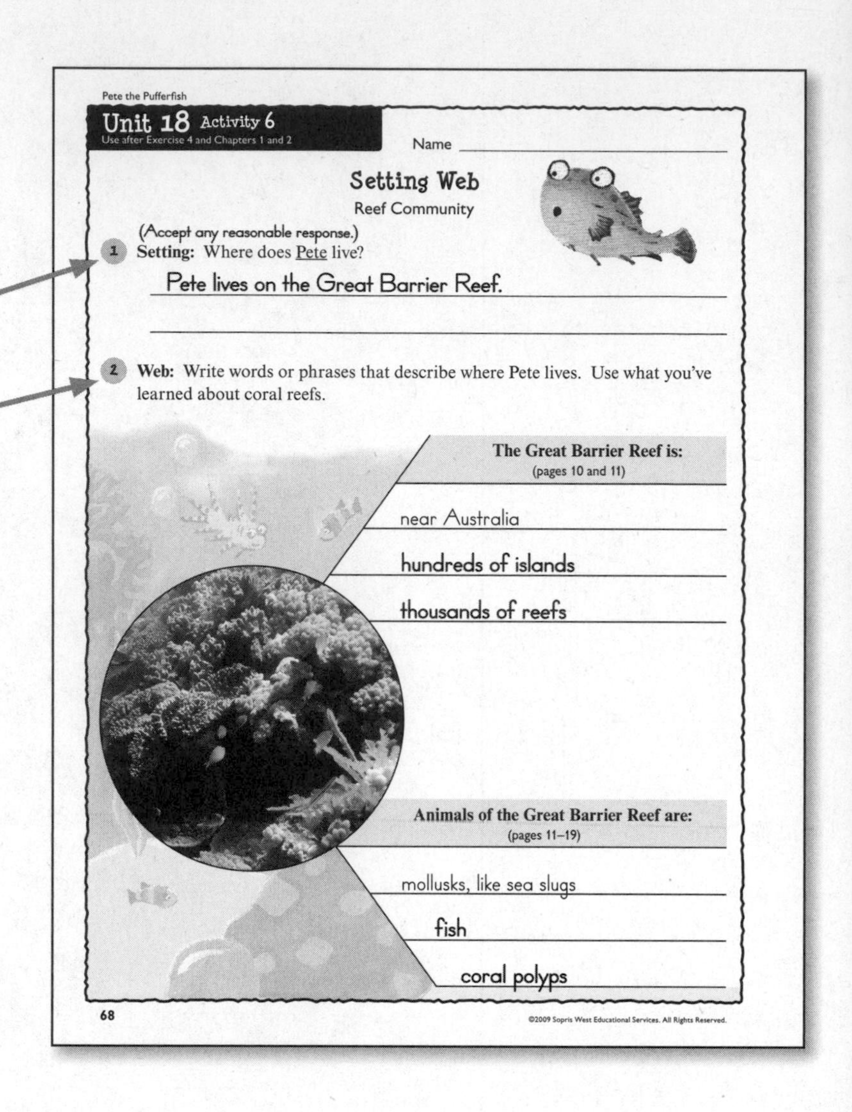

Pete the Pufferfish

Unit 18 Activity 6
Use after Exercise 4 and Chapters 1 and 2

Name ____________

Setting Web
Reef Community

(Accept any reasonable response.)

1 **Setting:** Where does Pete live?

Pete lives on the Great Barrier Reef.

2 **Web:** Write words or phrases that describe where Pete lives. Use what you've learned about coral reefs.

The Great Barrier Reef is:
(pages 10 and 11)

near Australia
hundreds of islands
thousands of reefs

Animals of the Great Barrier Reef are:
(pages 11–19)

mollusks, like sea slugs
fish
coral polyps

68

©2009 Sopris West Educational Services. All Rights Reserved.

PROCEDURES

For each step, demonstrate and guide practice, as needed. Then have students complete the page independently.

1. **Sentence Writing—Basic Instructions** (Item 1)
   Have students read the question and write a complete sentence, starting with "Pete lives . . . "
   Remind students to start sentences with a capital and end with a period.

2. **Setting: Web—Specific Instructions** (Item 2)
   Have students fill in the web by writing words that describe where Pete lives. Have students list and describe some of the animals at the reef. Remind them to look in their books for help if they need to.

Self-monitoring
Have students check and correct their work.

PASSAGE READING FLUENCY

FLUENCY

Accuracy, Expression, Rate

PROCEDURES

For each step, demonstrate and guide practice, as needed. Then have students complete the page independently.

Passage Reading—Basic Instructions

- Have students read the practice words.
- Have students finger track and whisper read the story two times—the first time for accuracy and the second time for expression. Have students cross out a letter each time they finish.
- Have students do a one-minute Timed Reading and cross out the timer.

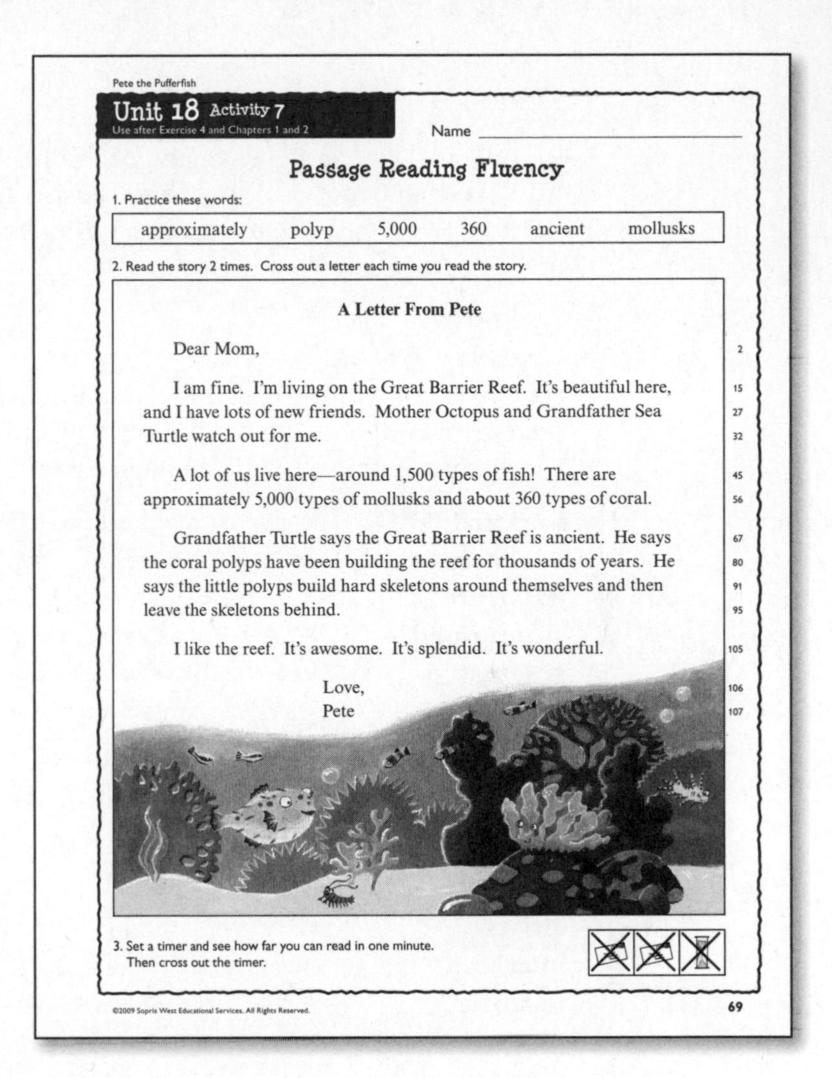

Pete the Pufferfish

Unit 18 Activity 7
Use after Exercise 4 and Chapters 1 and 2

Name ____________________

Passage Reading Fluency

1. Practice these words:

approximately	polyp	5,000	360	ancient	mollusks

2. Read the story 2 times. Cross out a letter each time you read the story.

A Letter From Pete

Dear Mom, 2

I am fine. I'm living on the Great Barrier Reef. It's beautiful here, 15
and I have lots of new friends. Mother Octopus and Grandfather Sea 27
Turtle watch out for me. 32

A lot of us live here—around 1,500 types of fish! There are 45
approximately 5,000 types of mollusks and about 360 types of coral. 56

Grandfather Turtle says the Great Barrier Reef is ancient. He says 67
the coral polyps have been building the reef for thousands of years. He 80
says the little polyps build hard skeletons around themselves and then 91
leave the skeletons behind. 95

I like the reef. It's awesome. It's splendid. It's wonderful. 105

Love, 106
Pete 107

3. Set a timer and see how far you can read in one minute.
Then cross out the timer.

69

PACING

Exercise 5a should take about 10 minutes, allowing about 10 minutes for the Focus Lesson.

BUILD ACCURACY AND FLUENCY (Reminder)

For all rows and columns, follow the specific directions, then build accuracy and fluency with whole words.

❶ SOUND REVIEW Use selected Sound Cards from Units 1–18.

❷ SHIFTY WORD BLENDING

❸ ACCURACY AND FLUENCY BUILDING

B1. Buildups

Tell students they can figure out bigger words by building from smaller words. Have students read the words. Assist, as needed.

Read the words. (or, tort; tort, contort; contort, contortion; contortion, contortionist)

A *contortionist* is a person who can twist his body into strange shapes.

C1. Multisyllabic Words

- For the list of words divided by syllables, have students read each syllable, then the whole word. Use the word in a sentence, as appropriate.
- For the list of whole words, build accuracy and then fluency.

forward	The opposite of backward is . . . *forward.*
adventures	Miss Tam has gone on many . . . *adventures.*
frustrated	When Joel couldn't climb the rope, he became . . . *frustrated.*
summoned	The Emperor . . . *summoned* . . . the people.
suggested	"Let's go for a walk after dinner," Mom . . . *suggested.*
confused	Please read the directions again. I'm . . . *confused.*

D1. Tricky Words

- For each Tricky Word, have students use the sounds and word parts they know to silently sound out the word. Use the word in a sentence to help with pronunciation.

gradually	Paula was very sick, then got better . . . *gradually.*
either	If Andrea's not going, I'm not going . . . *either.*
idea	The scientist had a brilliant . . . *idea.*
nothing	The opposite of everything is . . . *nothing.*
piece	After the pie was cut, Isabel gave everyone a . . . *piece.*
discouraged	Don't give up. Don't get . . . *discouraged.*

- Have students go back and read the whole words in the column.

❹ WORD ENDINGS

Have students read any underlined word, then the word with an ending.

Note: Tell students to note the spelling changes when endings are added to the words in Row B.

❺ NAMES

- Tell students these are characters they will read about in the story.
- Have students use the sounds and word parts they know to figure out the words. Use the words in sentences, as needed.

❻ MORPHOGRAPHS AND AFFIXES

- Have students read the underlined part, then the word.
- Repeat practice with whole words, mixing group and individual turns. Build accuracy, then fluency.

7 GENERALIZATION: READING NEW WORDS IN PARAGRAPHS

- Have students read the paragraph silently, then out loud. Tell students to use the sounds and word parts they know to read any difficult words.
- Repeat practice, as needed.

Pete the Pufferfish

Unit 18 Exercise 5a

Use before Chapters 3 and 4

1. SOUND REVIEW Use selected Sound Cards from Units 1–18.

2. SHIFTY WORD BLENDING For each word, have students say the underlined part, sound out smoothly, then read the word.

ink	sink	sank	stank	plank

3. ACCURACY/FLUENCY BUILDING For each column, have students say any underlined part, then read each word. Next, have them read the column.

A1 Mixed Practice	B1 Buildups	C1 Multisyllabic Words		D1 Tricky Words
circle	tort	for•ward	forward	gradually
escape	contort	ad•ven•tures	adventures	either
moment	contortion	frus•trat•ed	frustrated	idea
sore	contortionist	sum•moned	summoned	nothing
wedged		sug•gest•ed	suggested	piece
cause		con•fused	confused	discouraged

GRADUALLY INCREASE STUDENT RESPONSE RATE (Reminder)

After students are accurate, gradually increase the rate of response. Demonstrate and guide a pace slightly faster than the students' rate.

4. WORD ENDINGS Have students read any underlined word, then the word with an ending.

A	twisted		crooked	squirted		gulped
B	rub	rubbing	imagine	imagining	taste	tasty

5. NAMES Have students use the sounds and word parts they know to figure out the words.

Lady Ann	Mother Octopus	Grandfather Sea Turtle

6. MORPHOGRAPHS AND AFFIXES Have students read each underlined part, then the word.

A	reappeared	despite	coral	tightly
B	blindly	distressed	emptiness	became

7. GENERALIZATION Have students read the paragraph silently, then out loud. (New words: wriggled, ouch, normal)

Wiggly Phillip can twist his body into all kinds of shapes. He is a contortionist. Phillip walked up to a small box, balled up into a weird shape, and wriggled into the box. Ouch! That is certainly not normal. I wonder if it hurts.

SOPHISTICATED WORDS AND SENTENCES

FOCUS LESSON
Skills and Strategies

PURPOSE

The purpose of this lesson is to provide explicit instruction in identifying sophisticated word choices from synonyms. *Read Well* students have learned many advanced words and concepts. This lesson helps students be aware of their growing sophistication with words. The lesson also prepares students for Comprehension and Skill Work.

PREP NOTES
This is an oral lesson. An overhead is optional.

PACING
Exercise 5b should take about 10 minutes.

COMPREHENSION PROCESSES

Understand, Evaluate

PROCEDURES

❶ INTRODUCTION

Explain the purpose of the lesson. Say something like:

This Focus Lesson is about grown-up, or sophisticated, words. Say the word *sophisticated.* (sophisticated)
Sophisticated means . . . grown up.
I'm very proud of you because you've learned a lot of sophisticated words this year.
Read the paragraph above the gray bar. (Things that are grown-up are . . .)
Now read the sophisticated words in the gray bar. (commotion, bittersweet . . .)

❷ IDENTIFYING SOPHISTICATED WORDS AND SENTENCES

Using Vocabulary—bittersweet, integrity, exhausted, commotion; Making Judgments

- Guide students as they identify the most sophisticated sentence.

  Everyone, read the question. (Which sentence in the box is the most sophisticated?)
  Read Sentence 1. (When Miss Tam goes on a trip, she feels bittersweet.)
  Now read the underlined word. (bittersweet)
  Read Sentence 2. (When Miss Tam goes on a trip, she feels sad and glad.)
  Now read the underlined words. (sad and glad)
  Which sentence, Sentence 1 or 2, is a more sophisticated, or grown-up, way to describe how Miss Tam feels? (Sentence 1)
  That's right. Sentence 1 uses the sophisticated word for *sad and glad.*
  It uses the word . . . bittersweet.
  Read Sentence 1 again. (When Miss Tam goes on a trip, she feels bittersweet.)

  Let's try another one. Read Sentence 3. (The Emperor's successor had integrity.)
  Now read the underlined word. (integrity)
  Read Sentence 4.
  (The Emperor's successor was honest and did what was right.)
  Now read the underlined words. (honest and did what was right)
  Which sentence, Sentence 3 or 4, is a more sophisticated, or grown-up, way to describe the Emperor's successor? (Sentence 3)
  That's right. Sentence 3 uses the sophisticated word for *honest and did what was right.*
  It uses the word . . . integrity.
  Read Sentence 3 again. (The Emperor's successor had integrity.)

- Repeat with Sentences 5 and 6 and Sentences 7 and 8. If time allows, have students work in partners to determine which sentence in each pair is the most sophisticated.

Unit 18 Exercise 5b (Focus Lesson)
Use after Exercise 5a and before Chapters 3 and 4

Sophisticated Words and Sentences

Things that are grown-up are sophisticated. You've learned many sophisticated words in *Read Well.* The words in the gray bar are sophisticated words you've learned.

commotion **bittersweet** **exhausted** **integrity**

Which sentence in each box is the most sophisticated?

1. When Miss Tam goes on a trip, she feels bittersweet.
2. When Miss Tam goes on a trip, she feels sad and glad.

3. The Emperor's successor had integrity.
4. The Emperor's successor was honest and did what was right.

5. The dog detective was very tired.
6. The dog detective was exhausted.

7. Once at the big reef, Pete was amazed by all the commotion.
8. Once at the big reef, Pete was amazed by all the noise and activity.

COMPREHENSION PROCESSES

Understand, Apply

PROCEDURES

Introducing Vocabulary

★contortion ★frustrated
★confused

- For each vocabulary word, have students read the word by parts, then read the whole word.
- Read the student-friendly explanations to students as they follow with their fingers. Then have students use the vocabulary word by following the gray text.
- Review and discuss the photos and illustrations.

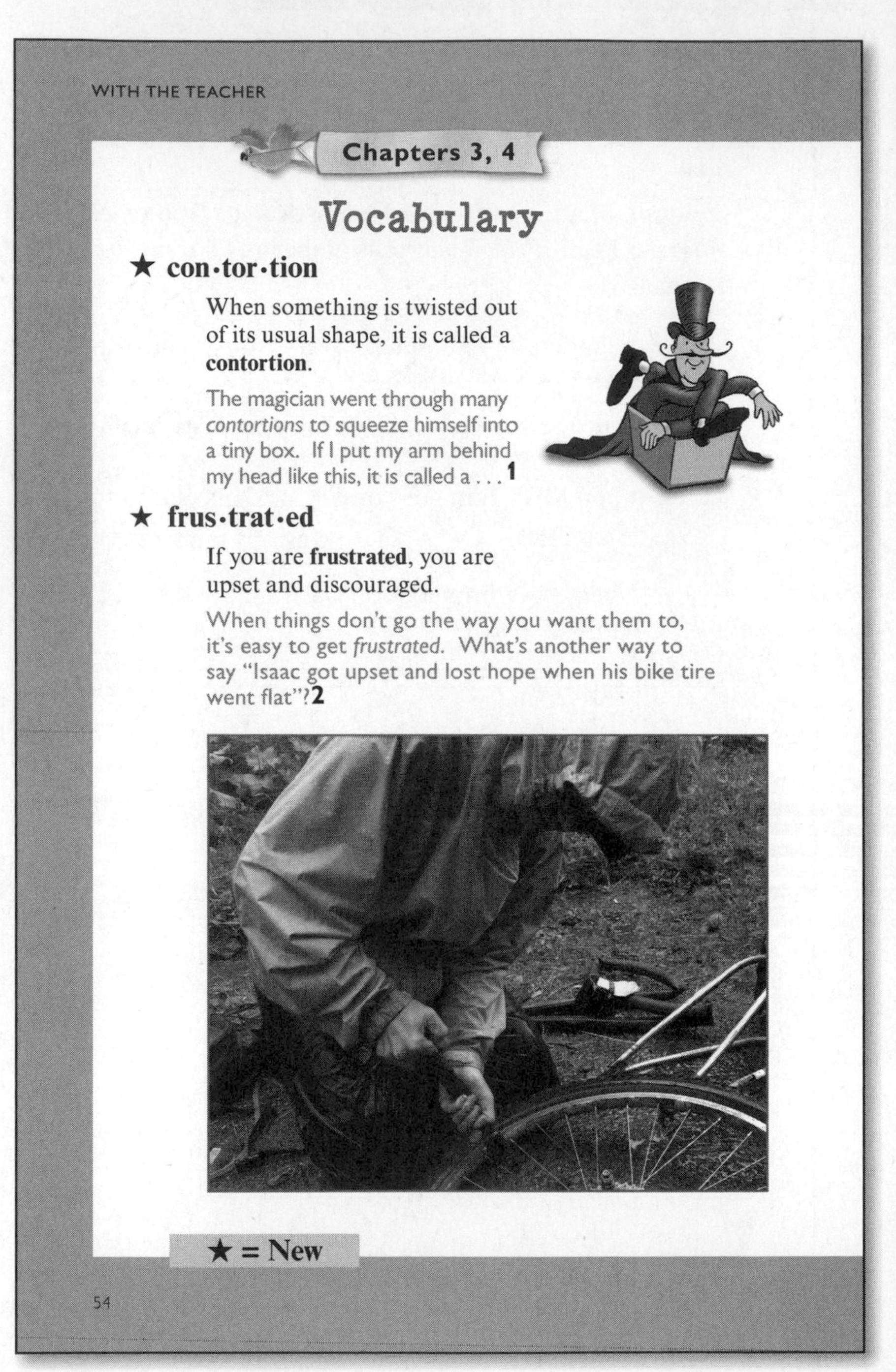
WITH THE TEACHER

Chapters 3, 4

Vocabulary

★ **con•tor•tion**

When something is twisted out of its usual shape, it is called a **contortion**.

The magician went through many *contortions* to squeeze himself into a tiny box. If I put my arm behind my head like this, it is called a . . . **1**

★ **frus•trat•ed**

If you are **frustrated**, you are upset and discouraged.

When things don't go the way you want them to, it's easy to get *frustrated*. What's another way to say "Isaac got upset and lost hope when his bike tire went flat"?**2**

★ = New

54

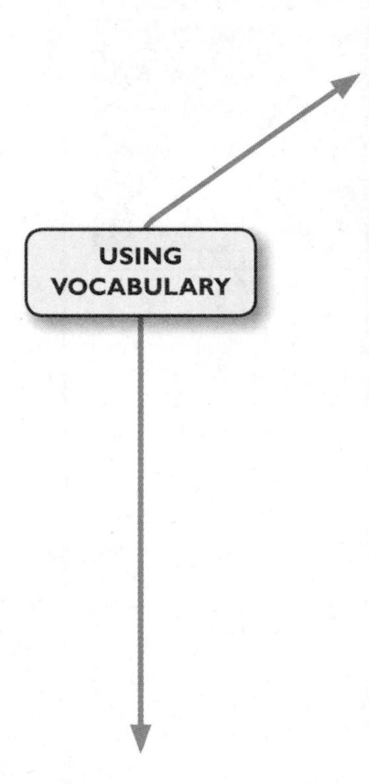

❶ **Understand:** Using Vocabulary—contortion (contortion)

❷ **Apply:** Using Vocabulary—frustrated (Isaac got frustrated when his bike tire went flat.)

★= New in this unit

★ **con·fused**

When you don't understand something, you are **confused**.

The road signs didn't match the map, and Mr. Chapman was *confused* about which way to go. Why was Mr. Chapman confused?[1]

USING VOCABULARY

❶ **Understand:** Using Vocabulary—confused (Mr. Chapman was confused because the road signs didn't match the map, and he didn't know which way to go.)

CHAPTER 3 INSTRUCTIONS

Students read Chapter 3 with the teacher and Chapter 4 on their own. *Note*: If you're working on an 8- to 11-Day Plan, you will read Chapter 4 with students.

COMPREHENSION PROCESSES

Remember, Understand, Apply

PROCEDURES

1. Reviewing Chapter 2

Summarizing; Using Vocabulary—advice, protect, flexible; Inferring

Have students turn to page 51. Quickly discuss the questions from Chapter 2, Setting a Purpose. Say something like:

Yesterday, you read Chapter 2 on your own. Let's see what you found out.

What was Mother Octopus's advice? (She told him to squeeze into a crack.)

Why was it hard for Pete to protect himself like Mother Octopus?

(Pete couldn't change his shape like Mother Octopus. His belly popped out when he let out his breath.)

Guide thinking. Say something like:

Mother Octopus thought Pete could protect himself by slipping into the crack in the rocks just like she did. Why can an octopus squeeze into small places?

(It has no bones.)

That's right! Why can't Pete do the same thing?

(He has bones. He is not as flexible.)

> **CORRECTING DECODING ERRORS**
>
> During story reading, gently correct any error, then have students reread the sentence.

2. Introducing Chapter 3

Identifying—Title; Predicting; Using Vocabulary—protect

Say something like:

Turn to page 56. What's the title of this chapter? (Try This!)

What do you think the chapter will be about?

(It will be about a new way for Pete to try to protect himself.)

3. First Reading

- Ask questions and discuss the text as indicated by the gray text.
- Mix group and individual turns, independent of your voice. Have students work toward a group accuracy goal of 0–4 errors. Quietly keep track of errors made by all students in the group.
- After reading the story, practice any difficult words. Repeat, if students have not reached the accuracy goal.

4. Second Reading, Short Passage Practice: Developing Prosody

- Demonstrate expressive, fluent reading of the first paragraph. Read at a rate slightly faster than the students' rate.
- Guide practice with your voice.
- Provide individual turns while others track with their fingers and whisper read.
- Repeat with one paragraph at a time.

Try This!

Poor Pete. He was stuck in a small crack in the rocks. He tried to wriggle out, but he was wedged so tightly that he couldn't move at all! "Uh, oh," said Pete. Grandfather Sea Turtle and Mother Octopus pushed on the rocks and tugged Pete's fins. Finally, he was free.

Pete rested on a piece of coral, rubbing his sore head and tail. "I am determined," Mother Octopus said. "Where there is a will, there is a way. Try this!" Then Mother Octopus squirted out a cloud of ink. From inside the black cloud, Mother Octopus said, "Ink will allow you to escape from a hungry predator. A big hungry fish can't see you through a cloud of black ink."

At that moment, Pete found himself lost in a sea of black. He couldn't see a thing. He swam blindly in a circle. "Ouch!" he yelled as he bumped into the reef.

PETE THE PUFFERFISH

Look at the pictures. Describe what's happening.[1]

57

COMPREHENDING AS YOU GO

1 Understand: Viewing, Describing, Sequencing (In the first picture, Mother Octopus and Grandfather Sea Turtle are trying to help get Pete out of the crack. In the second picture, Mother Octopus squirts out a cloud of black ink. In the third picture, Pete bumps into the reef because he can't see anything.)

WITH THE TEACHER

When the ink cleared, Grandfather Sea Turtle said, "Perhaps ink isn't the best idea for you either. We will just have to try something else." Then Grandfather Sea Turtle suggested they find a shell for Pete. "The big fish won't try to eat you if you have a shell."

Pete thought a shell was a great idea. They all swam around the reef looking for an empty shell that Pete could use. Some shells were too big; others were too small. Finally, they found a shell that was just right. Happily, Pete put the shell on his back, but it was so heavy that he sank to the ocean floor!

Nothing was working. Pete still didn't know how to protect himself.

Mother Octopus said, "Be back here at 6:00 a.m. I have another idea."

58

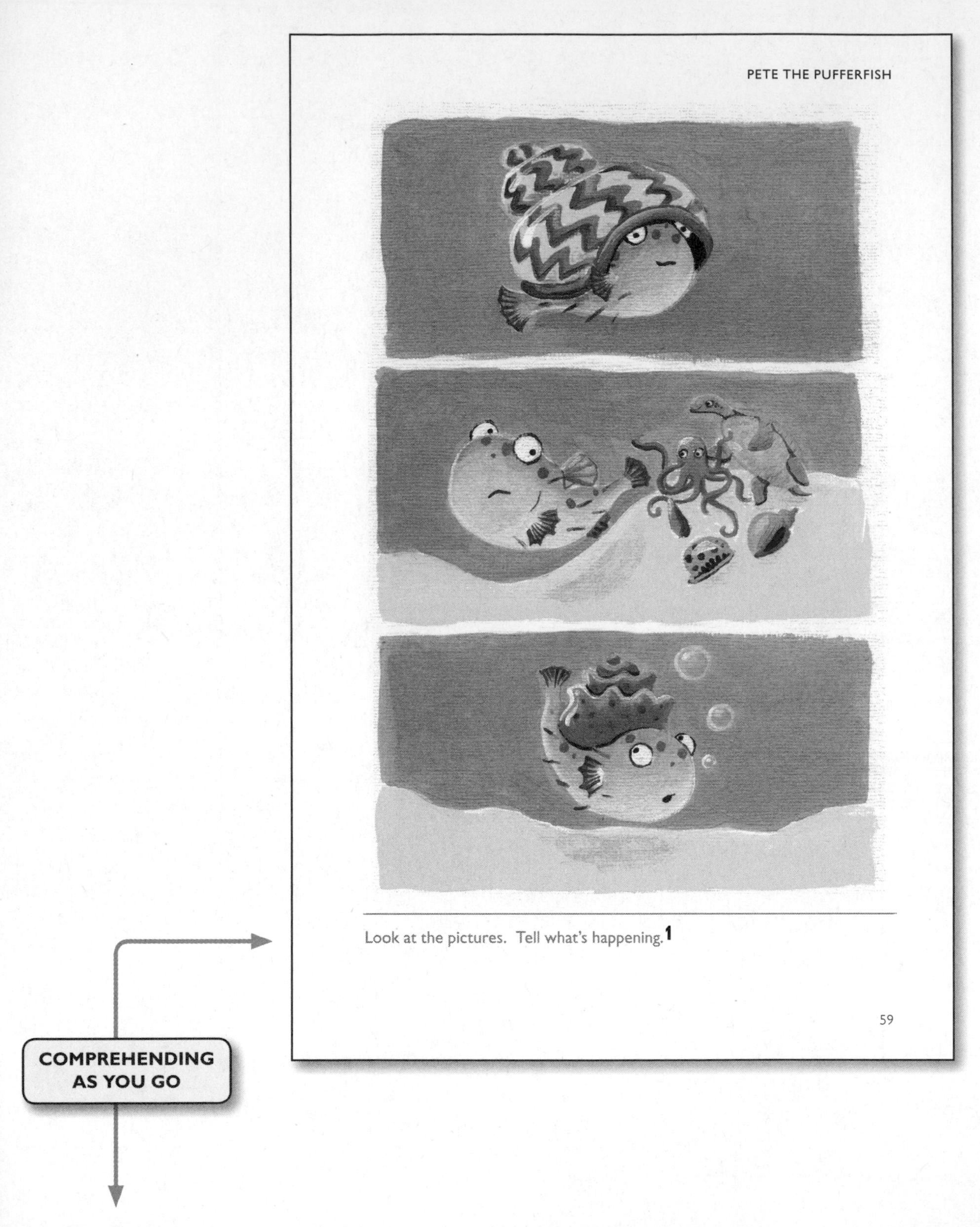

PETE THE PUFFERFISH

Look at the pictures. Tell what's happening.1

59

❶ **Understand:** Viewing, Describing, Sequencing (In the first picture, Pete is trying on a shell that is too big for him. In the second picture, Pete is looking for a new shell to try out. In the third picture, Pete is sinking to the ocean floor because the shell is too heavy.)

WITH THE TEACHER

GOAL

1. What does Pete need to learn to do?

CHARACTERS

2. Who are Pete's advisors?

ACTION

3. What were Mother Octopus's suggestions? Did they work?

ACTION

4. What was Grandfather Sea Turtle's suggestion? Did it work?

60

❶ **Understand:** Explaining—Goal; Using Vocabulary—protect (Pete needs to learn how to protect himself.)

❷ **Understand:** Identifying—Characters; Using Vocabulary—advisor (Pete's advisors are Mother Octopus and Grandfather Sea Turtle.)

❸ **Understand:** Summarizing—Action (Mother Octopus suggested that Pete hide in a crack. When that didn't work, she suggested that he squirt black ink. That didn't work either.)

❹ **Understand:** Summarizing—Action; Using Vocabulary—protect (Grandfather Sea Turtle suggested that Pete find a shell to protect himself with. When Pete found one his size, it was too heavy. He sank to the bottom of the ocean. The shell did not work.)

CHAPTER 4 INSTRUCTIONS

Students read without the teacher, independently or with partners.
Note: If you're working on an 8- to 11-Day Plan, you will read Chapter 4 with students.

COMPREHENSION PROCESSES

Understand

PROCEDURES FOR READING ON YOUR OWN

1. Getting Ready

Have students turn to Chapter 4 on page 61.

2. Setting a Purpose

Explaining; Using Vocabulary—protect

Before students begin reading, say something like:

Read to find out the answers to these questions:

- How does Lady Ann protect herself?
- What is the happy ending?

> **PREP NOTE**
> **Setting a Purpose**
> Write questions on a chalkboard, white board, or large piece of paper before working with your small group.

3. Reading on Your Own: Partner or Whisper Reading

- Have students take turns reading every other page with a partner or have students whisper read on their own.
- Continue having students track each word with their fingers.
- Have students ask themselves or their partners the gray text questions.

4. Comprehension and Skill Work

For students on a 6-Day Plan, tell them they will do Comprehension and Skill Activities 8 and 9 after they read on their own. Guide practice, as needed. For teacher directions, see pages 111 and 112. (For 8- to 11-Day Plans, see the Lesson Planner, page 9.)

5. Homework 5: Repeated Reading

Pete's Trick

In the morning, Pete and Grandfather Sea Turtle met at the fire coral. Mother Octopus had summoned Lady Ann the Seahorse. Mother Octopus said, "Lady Ann came all the way from the seagrass to help. She can show Pete how to protect himself from the big fish!"

Without a word, Lady Ann swam to a patch of purple fire coral and disappeared. Pete was amazed. "I want to learn that trick!" said Pete.

Lady Ann gradually reappeared. "I know no tricks," said Lady Ann. "When I swim in front of something, I change colors to match it. Perhaps if you looked more like me, you could do this as well."

Pete gave it a try. He screwed up his nose, swam upright like the horse, and crooked his tail. Despite all his contortions, his color didn't change.

What was Lady Ann's suggestion? [1] Did this work for Pete? [2]

COMPREHENDING AS YOU GO

❶ **Understand:** Explaining (Lady Ann suggested that Pete try to make himself change color to match things around him.)

❷ **Understand:** Explaining (No, he tried to make himself like a seahorse, but he couldn't change color.)

Imagining himself in the belly of a shark, Pete became quite distressed. Nothing was working. He was so frustrated that he gulped some water and let it out again with a sigh. Mother Octopus looked at Pete. "That's it!" she said. "You did it. You can protect yourself. Do it again."

Pete looked confused. "Do what?" he asked.

Grandfather Sea Turtle said, "Do what you did just before you sighed."

Pete still looked confused, but he sucked in a huge gulp of water.

"Look," said Mother Octopus. "Look! Your spines are sticking out, and you are big, fat, and round! No fish will try to eat you like that!" Pete was surprised to see that his spines were sticking out and his body had puffed up like a balloon. Pete let out the water with an excited whoosh.

ON YOUR OWN

Then Pete sucked in an even bigger gulp of water. His body puffed up to three times its normal size!

Grandfather Sea Turtle chuckled as he looked at Pete's spines. "Any big fish that thinks you will be a tasty little snack will be in for a big surprise."

From that day forward, Pete had many more adventures with his friends on the reef, but he never forgot the day that he learned how to be Pete the Pufferfish.

Describe how Pete protects himself.[1]

64

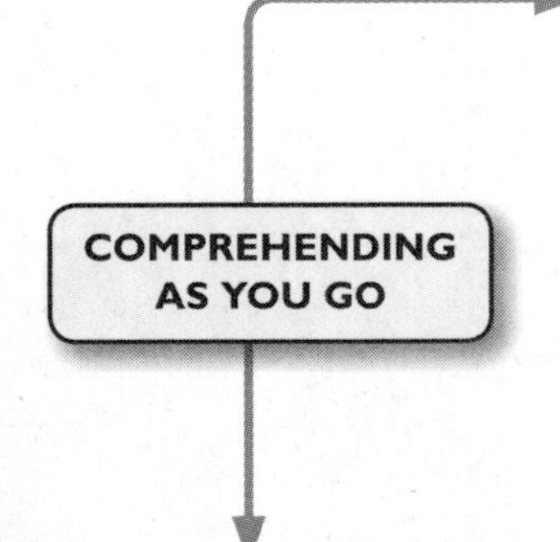

1 Understand: Describing; Using Vocabulary—protect (To protect himself, Pete sucks in big gulps of water that make him puff up with his spines sticking out. When he is big like that, no other fish wants to eat him.)

SNAZZY WORDS AND SOPHISTICATED SENTENCES

SNAZZY WORDS AND SYNONYMS

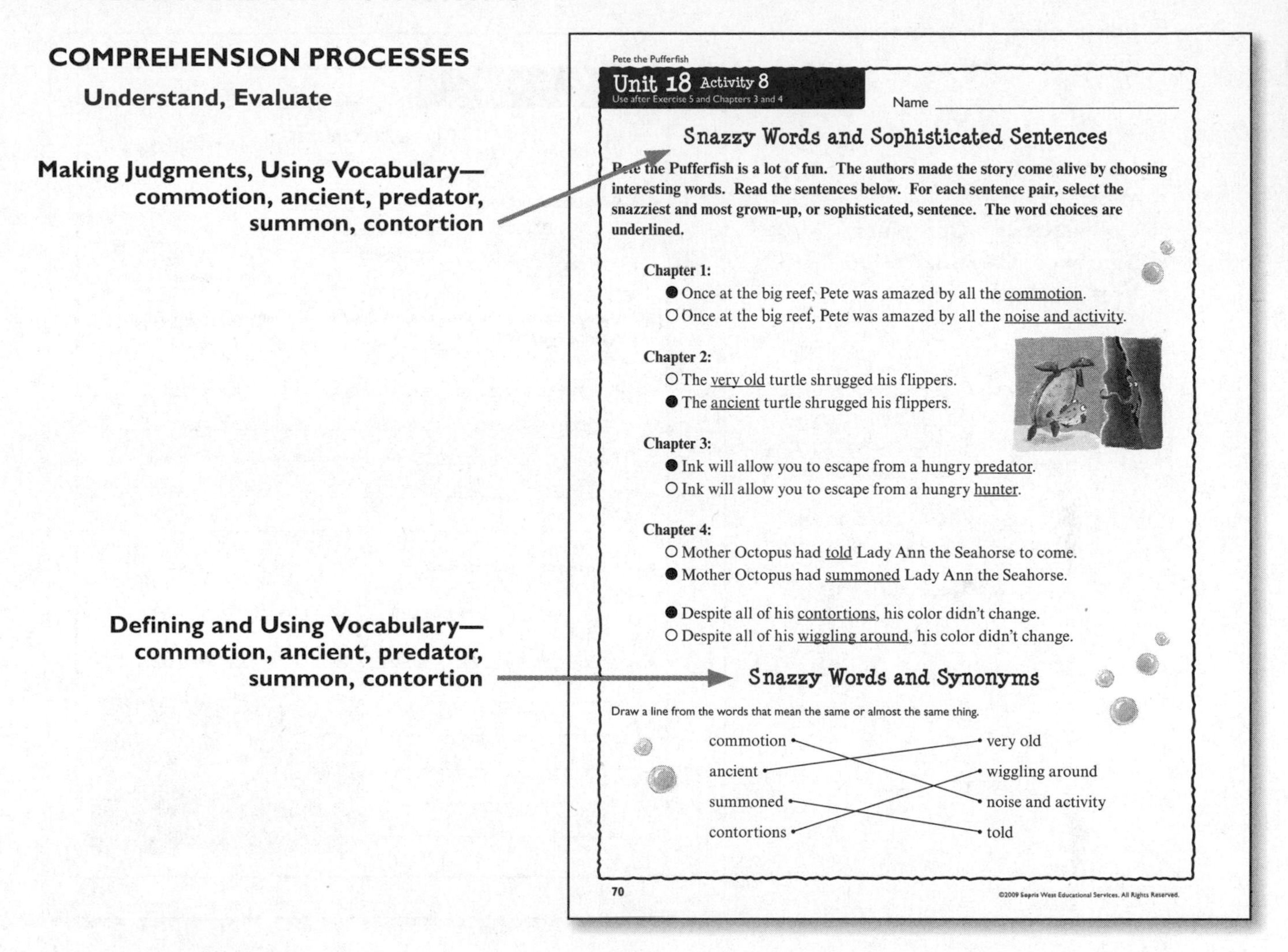

COMPREHENSION PROCESSES

Understand, Evaluate

Making Judgments, Using Vocabulary—commotion, ancient, predator, summon, contortion

Defining and Using Vocabulary—commotion, ancient, predator, summon, contortion

Pete the Pufferfish

Unit 18 Activity 8
Use after Exercise 5 and Chapters 3 and 4

Name ____________________

Snazzy Words and Sophisticated Sentences

Pete the Pufferfish is a lot of fun. The authors made the story come alive by choosing interesting words. Read the sentences below. For each sentence pair, select the snazziest and most grown-up, or sophisticated, sentence. The word choices are underlined.

Chapter 1:
● Once at the big reef, Pete was amazed by all the commotion.
○ Once at the big reef, Pete was amazed by all the noise and activity.

Chapter 2:
○ The very old turtle shrugged his flippers.
● The ancient turtle shrugged his flippers.

Chapter 3:
● Ink will allow you to escape from a hungry predator.
○ Ink will allow you to escape from a hungry hunter.

Chapter 4:
○ Mother Octopus had told Lady Ann the Seahorse to come.
● Mother Octopus had summoned Lady Ann the Seahorse.

● Despite all of his contortions, his color didn't change.
○ Despite all of his wiggling around, his color didn't change.

Snazzy Words and Synonyms

Draw a line from the words that mean the same or almost the same thing.

commotion	very old
ancient	wiggling around
summoned	noise and activity
contortions	told

70

©2009 Sopris West Educational Services. All Rights Reserved.

PROCEDURES

For each step, demonstrate and guide practice, as needed. Then have students complete the page independently.

Snazzy Words and Sophisticated Sentences: Selection Response—Specific Instructions

Have students read the sentence pairs, then fill in the bubble for the sentence that is the most sophisticated.

Snazzy Words and Synonyms: Selection Response—Specific Instructions

Have students read the words in the first column, then choose a word or phrase from the second column that means the same. Have them draw a line between the synonyms.

CHARACTERIZATION

COMPREHENSION PROCESSES

Remember, Understand, Evaluate, Create

WRITING TRAITS

Ideas and Content
Word Choice
Conventions—Complete Sentence, Capital, Period
Presentation

Identifying—Character Traits (Characterization); Using Vocabulary—determined, ravenous, extinct, spunky, herbivore, omnivore

Explaining—Character Traits (Characterization), Sentence Writing

Responding, Generating Ideas Sentence Writing

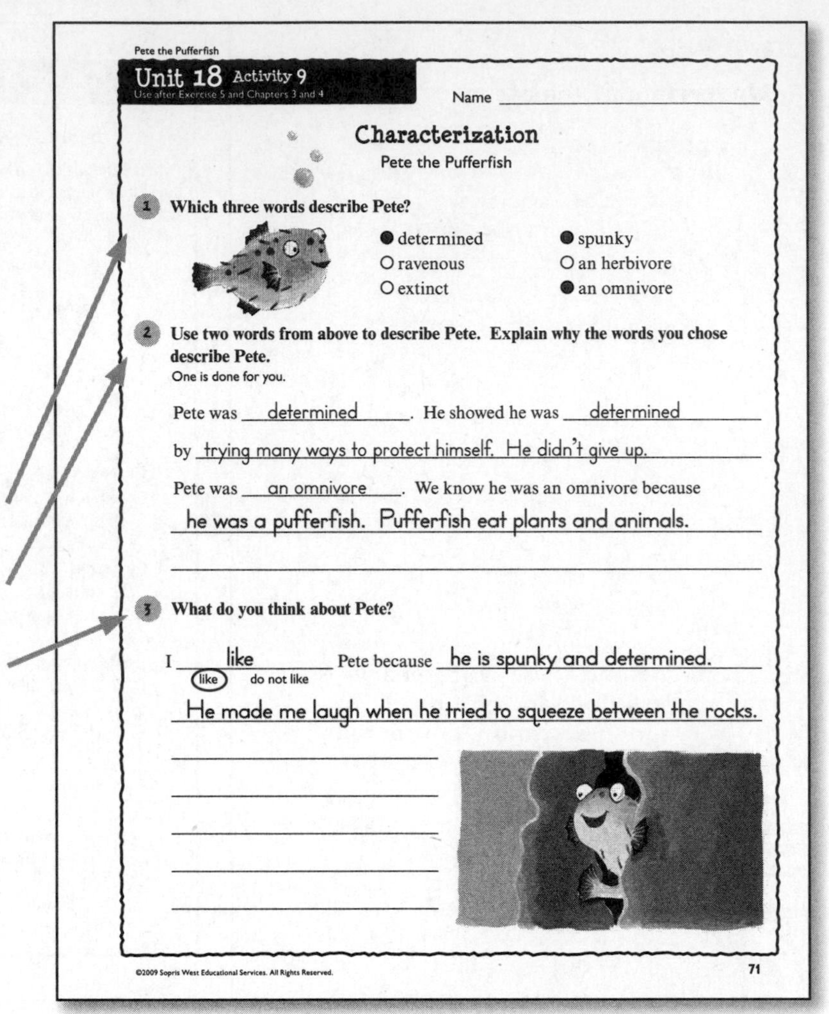

Pete the Pufferfish

Unit 18 Activity 9
Use after Exercise 5 and Chapters 3 and 4

Name ______

Characterization
Pete the Pufferfish

1. **Which three words describe Pete?**

● determined ○ ravenous ○ extinct
● spunky ○ an herbivore ● an omnivore

2. **Use two words from above to describe Pete. Explain why the words you chose describe Pete.**
One is done for you.

Pete was determined. He showed he was determined by trying many ways to protect himself. He didn't give up.

Pete was an omnivore. We know he was an omnivore because he was a pufferfish. Pufferfish eat plants and animals.

3. **What do you think about Pete?**

I like (like / do not like) Pete because he is spunky and determined. He made me laugh when he tried to squeeze between the rocks.

©2009 Sopris West Educational Services. All Rights Reserved.

71

PROCEDURES

For each step, demonstrate and guide practice, as needed. Then have students complete the page independently.

1. **Selection Response—Specific Instructions** (Item 1)
   Have students fill in the bubbles for three words that describe Pete the Pufferfish.

2. **Description: Paragraph Writing—Specific Instructions** (Item 2)
   Have students read the directions, then write a paragraph that describes Pete. Remind them to use the words they selected in Item 1 and to use capitals and periods.

3. **Personal Response: Paragraph Writing—Specific Instructions** (Item 3)
   Have students read the directions, then write a personal response telling why they like or do not like the character Pete.

JUST FOR FUN • AUTHORS' CORNER

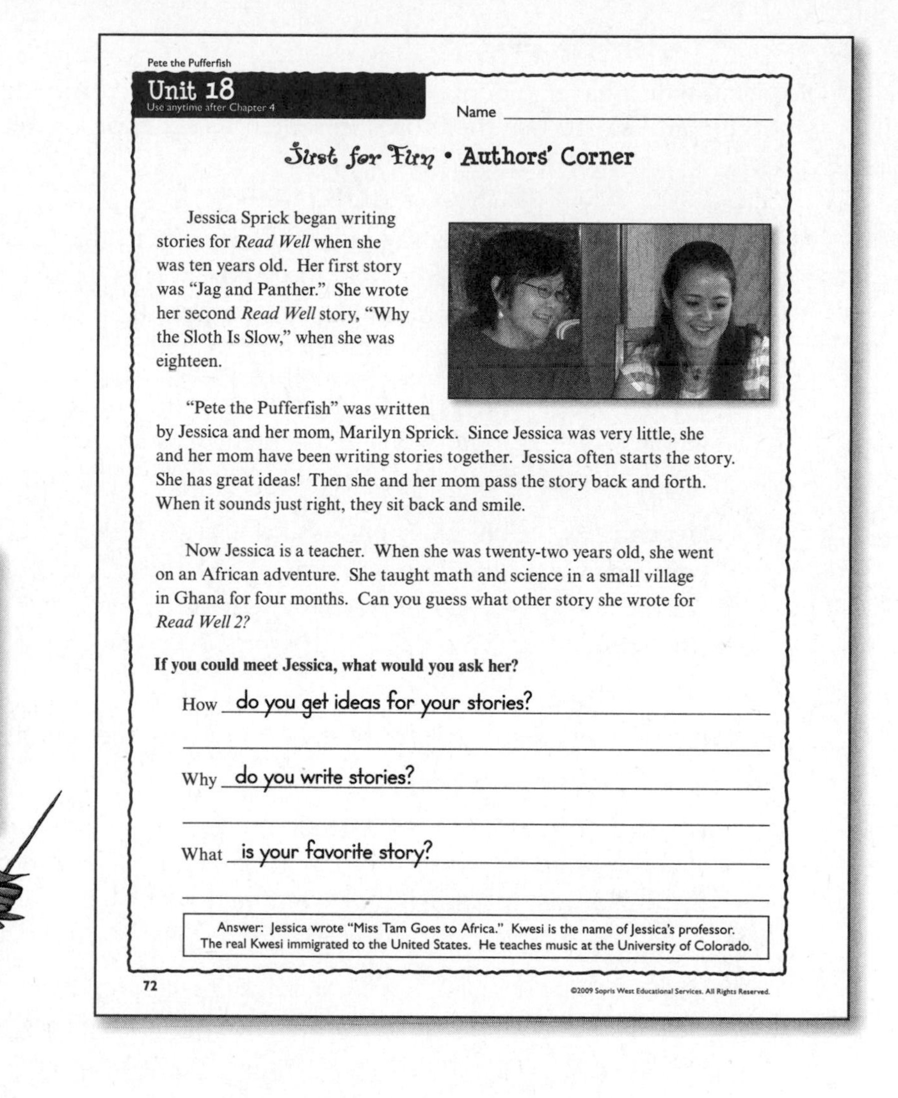

Pete the Pufferfish

Unit 18
Use anytime after Chapter 4

Name ____________________

Just for Fun • Authors' Corner

Jessica Sprick began writing stories for *Read Well* when she was ten years old. Her first story was "Jag and Panther." She wrote her second *Read Well* story, "Why the Sloth Is Slow," when she was eighteen.

"Pete the Pufferfish" was written by Jessica and her mom, Marilyn Sprick. Since Jessica was very little, she and her mom have been writing stories together. Jessica often starts the story. She has great ideas! Then she and her mom pass the story back and forth. When it sounds just right, they sit back and smile.

Now Jessica is a teacher. When she was twenty-two years old, she went on an African adventure. She taught math and science in a small village in Ghana for four months. Can you guess what other story she wrote for *Read Well 2?*

If you could meet Jessica, what would you ask her?

How do you get ideas for your stories?

Why do you write stories?

What is your favorite story?

Answer: Jessica wrote "Miss Tam Goes to Africa." Kwesi is the name of Jessica's professor. The real Kwesi immigrated to the United States. He teaches music at the University of Colorado.

72

HOW TO USE "JUST FOR FUN" ACTIVITIES

Note: This activity is optional and is *just for fun.* Use the activity:
- as a cushion activity
- for homework
- just for fun

PROCEDURES

As time allows, have students read the information about the authors, then write questions they would like to ask the authors. This page may be given to students as homework.

❶ SOUND REVIEW

Have students read the sounds and key word phrases. Work for accuracy, then fluency.

❷ SHIFTY WORD BLENDING

For each word, have students say the underlined sound. Then have them sound out the word smoothly and say it. Use the words in sentences, as appropriate.

❸ ACCURACY AND FLUENCY BUILDING

- For each task, have students say any underlined part, then read the word.
- Set a pace. Then have students read the whole words in each task and column.
- Provide repeated practice, building accuracy first, then fluency.

C1. Multisyllabic Words

- For the list of words divided by syllables, have students read each syllable, then the whole word. Use the word in a sentence, as appropriate.
- For the list of whole words, build accuracy and then fluency.

Bertha My favorite aunt's name is . . . *Bertha.*
yesterday The little boy cleaned his room . . . *yesterday.*
scuba Would you like to . . . *scuba* . . . dive?
librarian The person in charge of the library is the . . . *librarian.*

D1. Rhyming Words

Have students read each set of rhyming words and identify what's the same about them.

E1. Tricky Words

- For each Tricky Word, have students use the sounds and word parts they know to silently sound out the word. Use the word in a sentence to help with pronunciation.
- If the word is unfamiliar, tell students the word.

journal
Look at the first word. Say the word parts silently. Thumbs up when you know the word. Use my sentence to help you pronounce the word. Every day the author writes in a . . . *journal.* Read the word three times. (journal, journal, journal)

among The stinkbugs live . . . *among* . . . the weeds.
pears My favorite fruits are grapes, apples, and . . . *pears.*

- Have students go back and read the whole words in the column.

❹ MORPHOGRAPHS AND AFFIXES

- Have students read "pre = before" and the accompanying word and sentence. Then have students explain the sentence. Repeat with "re = again."
- For Row C, have students read the underlined part, then the word.
- Repeat practice with whole words, mixing group and individual turns. Build accuracy, then fluency.

❺ GENERALIZATION: READING NEW WORDS IN PARAGRAPHS

- Have students read the paragraph silently, then out loud. Tell students to use the sounds and word parts they know to read any difficult words.
- Repeat practice, as needed.

Fluency

Unit 18 Exercise 6

Use before Miss Tam Goes Home

1. SOUND REVIEW Have students review sounds for accuracy, then for fluency.

A	ge	ph	u_e	ci	kn
B	ue	ce	igh	i_e	gi

2. SHIFTY WORD BLENDING For each word, have students say the underlined part, sound out smoothly, then read the word.

ice	dice	dive	live	life

3. ACCURACY/FLUENCY BUILDING For each column, have students say any underlined part, then read each word. Next, have them read the column.

A1 Mixed Practice	B1 Compound Words	C1 Multisyllabic Words	D1 Rhyming Words	E1 Tricky Words
boots	sheepskin	Ber•tha	delicious	journal
pages	clownfish	yes•ter•day	luscious	among
eels	parrotfish	scu•ba	scrumptious	pears
moray	wetsuit	li•brar•i•an		**E2** Names & Places
photos	**B2** Word Endings	Bertha	pictures	Australia
Aussies	flipped	yesterday	creatures	Montgomery
gear	grinned	scuba	adventures	Alabama
Paddy	swimming	librarian		Ghana
thirty				Hawaii

MONITORING PROGRESS

For all activities, mix group and individual turns to keep students engaged and to monitor individual performance.

4. MORPHOGRAPHS AND AFFIXES Have students practice reading "pre = before" and "re = again" and the related words and sentences. For Row C, have students read each underlined part, then the word.

A	pre = before	preview = view before	The teacher will preview the movie.
B	re = again	review = view again	The teacher will review my report.

C	recalled	music	vision	needless	coral

5. GENERALIZATION Have students read the paragraph silently, then out loud. (New words: recipe, stairs, taxi)

Miss Tam decided to invite Mr. Moffitt and Bertha over for tacos, fruit salad, and a tasty lemon pudding. She had a pudding recipe given to her by a friend. She needed vanilla and cream, so she quickly got dressed, toddled down the stairs of her home, and called a taxi to go shopping. "Oh my," said Miss Tam. "My friends will be here soon. I really have to hurry!"

FLUENCY PASSAGE INSTRUCTIONS

This Story Reading targets fluency as the primary goal of instruction and practice. Students do repeated readings of this poem to improve accuracy, expression, and rate.

PROCEDURES

1. Warm-Up: Partner Reading or Whisper Reading

Before beginning group Story Reading, have students finger track and partner or whisper read the selection.

> **PARTNER READING—CHECKOUT OPPORTUNITY**
>
> While students are Partner Reading, listen to individuals read the passage. Work on accuracy and fluency, as needed.

2. First Reading

- Mix group and individual turns, independent of your voice. Have students work toward a group accuracy goal of 0–4 errors. Quietly keep track of errors made by all students in the group.
- After reading the story, practice any difficult words. Reread the story if students have not reached the accuracy goal.

3. Second Reading, Short Passage Practice: Developing Prosody

- Demonstrate reading the first paragraph with expression and fluency. Have students finger track as you read.
- Have students choral read the first paragraph. Encourage reading with expression and fluency.
- Repeat with second paragraph.

4. Third Reading, Group Timed Readings: Repeated Reading

- Select a page. Encourage each child to work for a personal best. Have students whisper read for a one-minute Timed Reading. Tell students to go back to the top of the page and keep reading until the minute is up.
- Have students put their finger on the last word they read and count the number of words read correctly in one minute.
- Have students do a second Timed Reading of the same page.
- Have students try to beat their last score.
- Celebrate improvements.

5. Written Assessment (Comprehension and Skill)

Tell students they will do a Written Assessment after they read "Miss Tam Goes Home." (For teacher directions, see pages 120–122.)

6. Homework 6: Repeated Reading

WITH THE TEACHER

Fluency

Miss Tam Goes Home

by Ann Watanabe
illustrated by Page Eastburn O'Rourke

"Life is an adventure," thought Miss Tam as she settled into seat 17B and got ready for the long airplane ride home. Just like her trips to Ghana and Hawaii, Miss Tam's time in Australia had gone by quickly. 7 18 27 35 39

It seemed like it was just yesterday that she had retired from her job as a children's librarian in Montgomery, Alabama. But here she was, several months later, returning home from her third grand adventure. 48 57 64 71 74

65

WITH THE TEACHER

Fluency

Miss Tam pulled out her tattered journal. 7
She flipped through the pages and reviewed 14
her notes and photos. She recalled shopping 21
at Paddy's Market. "Great fruits, vegetables, 27
music, and people," she thought. "Bertha will 34
love my sheepskin boots! Oh, and I can't wait 43
to give Minnie Bird and Old Scraggly Cat 51
their gifts!" 53

Miss Tam flipped a page and read her 61
notes about the lemon rice pudding with 68
pears and vanilla ice cream. "Luscious, 74
delicious," thought Miss Tam. "I will have to 82
get the recipe." 85

66

Miss Tam smiled as she looked through page after page of pictures and notes. When she got to the pages about her dive at the Great Barrier Reef, she grinned from ear to ear. She chuckled as she looked at the underwater photos of herself in pink fins, face mask, wetsuit, and scuba gear. There she was, swimming among parrotfish, clownfish, moray eels, and living coral. Before she knew it, Miss Tam was in a deep sleep. 8 17 27 36 44 52 59 65 75 77

Thirty hours later, Miss Tam was getting out of a taxi in front of her home. She toddled up the stairs, opened the door, and exclaimed, "Hooly-dooly!" 84 95 103 105

"Hooly-dooly!" screeched Minnie Bird. 110

WRITTEN ASSESSMENT (1 of 3)

COMPREHENSION PROCESSES

Remember, Understand, Apply

WRITING TRAITS

Organization—Topic Sentence, Supporting Details
Word Choice
Conventions—Complete Sentence, Capital, Period
Presentation

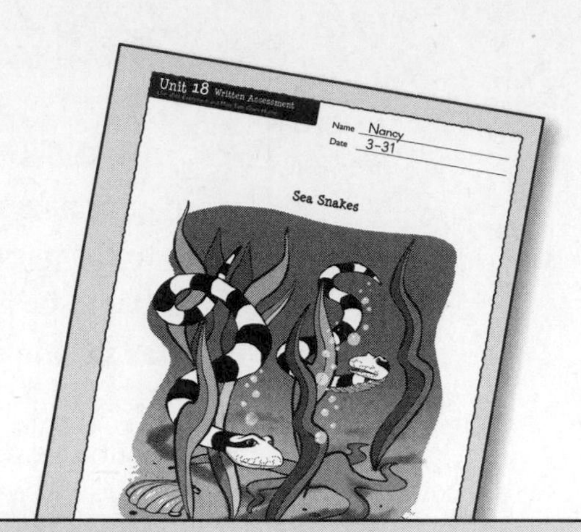

Test Taking → **Unit 18** Written Assessment
Use after Exercise 6 and Miss Tam Goes Home

WARM-UP

carnivores	approximately	paddle	poisonous

Sea Snakes

You might have read about snakes that live on land. But did you know that there are approximately 70 different kinds of snakes that live in the ocean?

Sea snakes look a lot like their land relatives, yet they are different. Most sea snakes have a tail that is shaped like a paddle, and their bodies are flatter than land snakes. These things help them to swim. Most sea snakes can't move on land at all.

Like all reptiles, sea snakes breathe air. They come to the surface to breathe. They can also get air from the water through their skins. Sea snakes can stay underwater for as long as two hours.

Sea snakes are carnivores. They hunt for fish by poking their heads into cracks and holes where fish are hiding. Their bite is poisonous. Luckily for us, they don't usually bite people!

continued

120

WRITTEN ASSESSMENT (2 of 3)

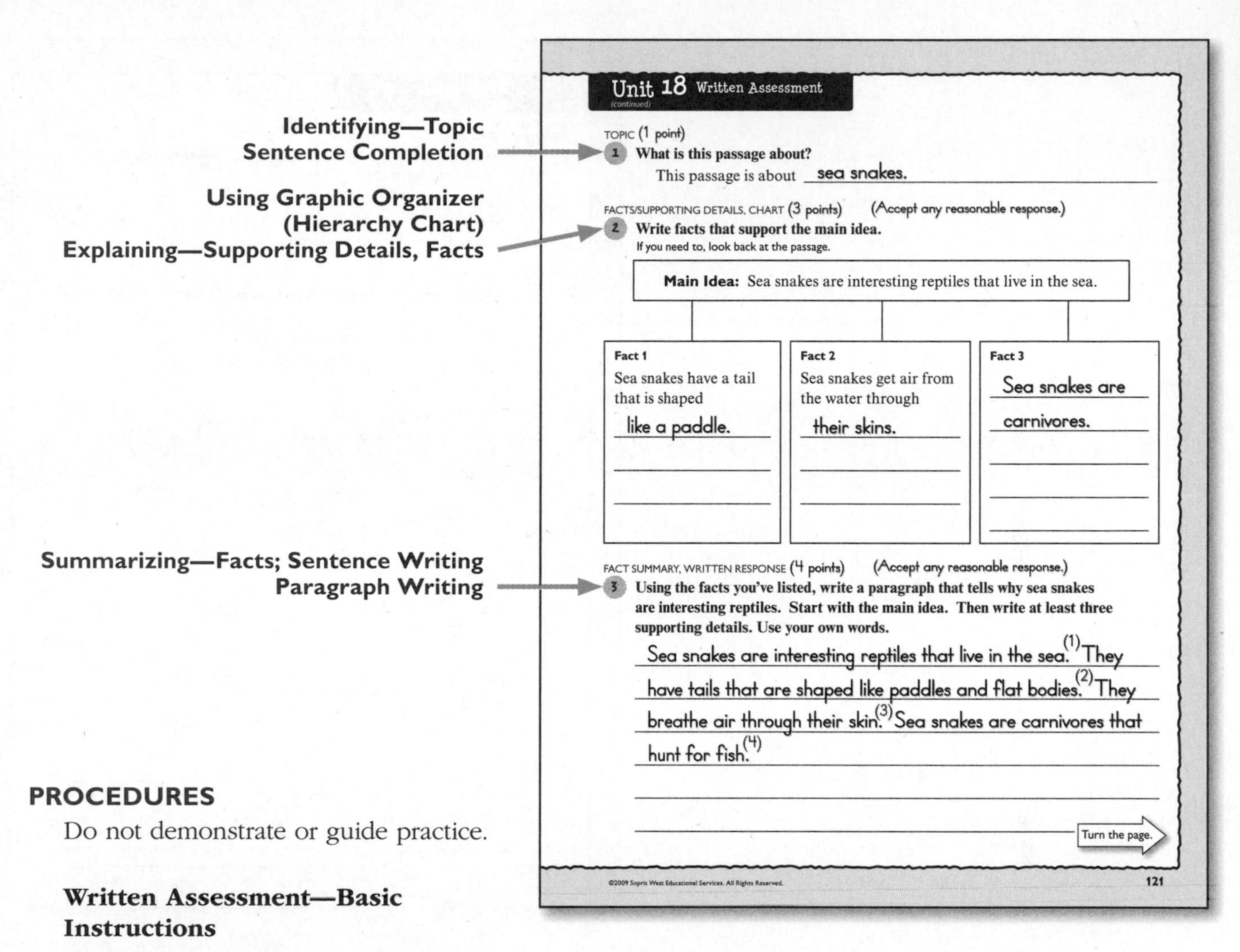

Unit 18 Written Assessment (continued)

TOPIC (1 point)

1 **What is this passage about?**

This passage is about sea snakes.

FACTS/SUPPORTING DETAILS, CHART (3 points) (Accept any reasonable response.)

2 **Write facts that support the main idea.**
If you need to, look back at the passage.

Main Idea: Sea snakes are interesting reptiles that live in the sea.

Fact 1	Fact 2	Fact 3
Sea snakes have a tail that is shaped like a paddle.	Sea snakes get air from the water through their skins.	Sea snakes are carnivores.

FACT SUMMARY, WRITTEN RESPONSE (4 points) (Accept any reasonable response.)

3 **Using the facts you've listed, write a paragraph that tells why sea snakes are interesting reptiles. Start with the main idea. Then write at least three supporting details. Use your own words.**

Sea snakes are interesting reptiles that live in the sea.(1) They have tails that are shaped like paddles and flat bodies.(2) They breathe air through their skin.(3) Sea snakes are carnivores that hunt for fish.(4)

Turn the page.

 121

PROCEDURES

Do not demonstrate or guide practice.

Written Assessment—Basic Instructions

1. Introduce the Written Assessment.
   - Tell students that their work today is an opportunity for them to show what they can do independently. Say something like:
     You should be very proud of your accomplishments. Remember, on a Written Assessment, you get to show me what you can do all by yourself.
   - Tell students they will whisper read the passage and then answer the questions without help.

2. Check for student understanding.
   Say something like:
   Look at your assessment. What are you going to do first? (write my name)

   What are going to do next? (whisper read the passage)
   What will you do after you read the passage? (answer the questions)

   That's great. Now what will you do if you get to a hard question?
   (reread the question and try again)
   That's right. What should you do if it's still hard? (reread the passage and try again)
   Very good. And if you still aren't sure, what will you do? (do my best and keep going)

WRITTEN ASSESSMENT (3 of 3)

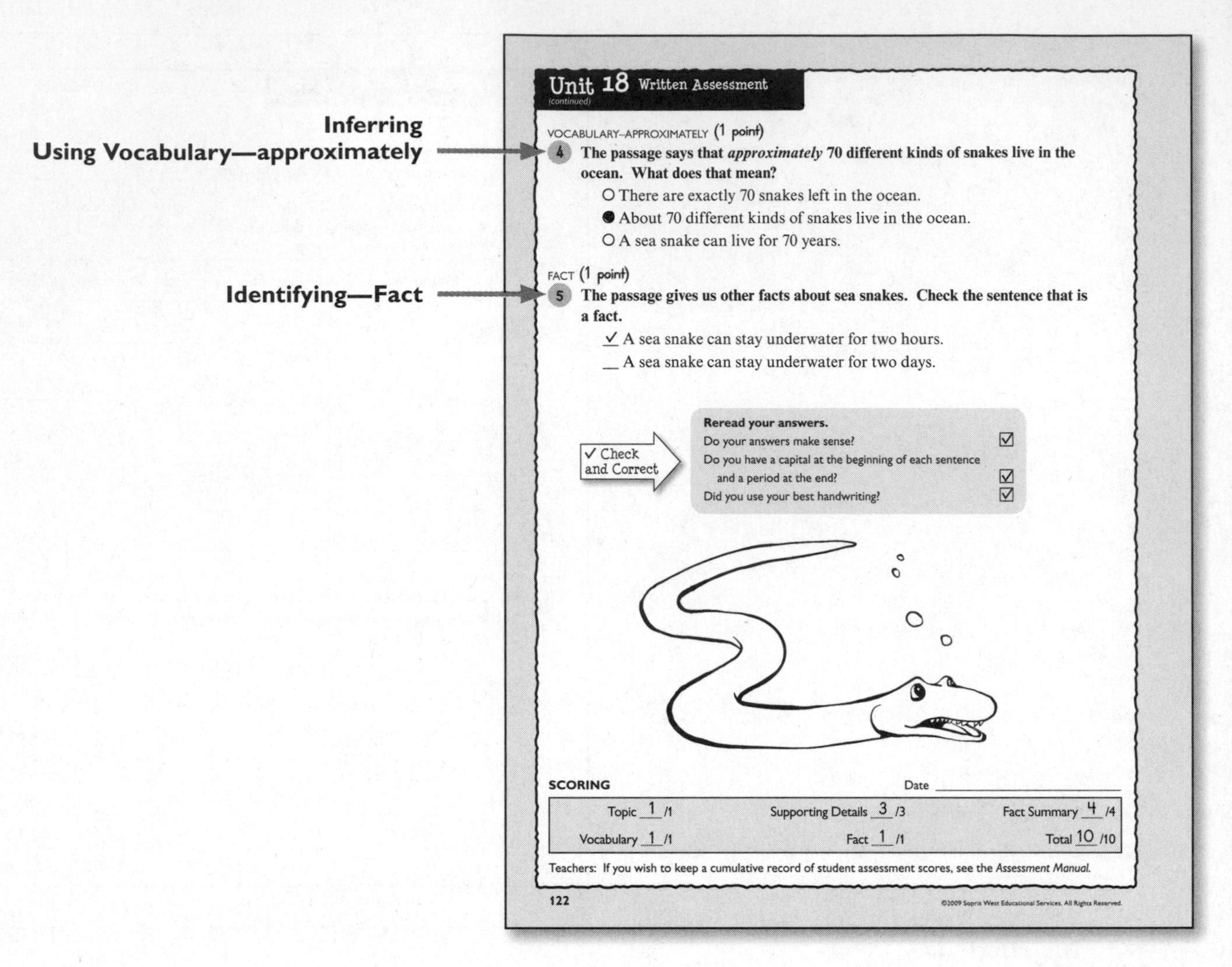

Unit 18 Written Assessment
(continued)

VOCABULARY–APPROXIMATELY (1 point)

4. **The passage says that *approximately* 70 different kinds of snakes live in the ocean. What does that mean?**
   - ○ There are exactly 70 snakes left in the ocean.
   - ● About 70 different kinds of snakes live in the ocean.
   - ○ A sea snake can live for 70 years.

FACT (1 point)

5. **The passage gives us other facts about sea snakes. Check the sentence that is a fact.**
   - ✓ A sea snake can stay underwater for two hours.
   - __ A sea snake can stay underwater for two days.

✓ Check and Correct

Reread your answers.
- Do your answers make sense? ☑
- Do you have a capital at the beginning of each sentence and a period at the end? ☑
- Did you use your best handwriting? ☑

SCORING Date ____________

Topic 1 /1	Supporting Details 3 /3	Fact Summary 4 /4
Vocabulary 1 /1	Fact 1 /1	Total 10 /10

Teachers: If you wish to keep a cumulative record of student assessment scores, see the *Assessment Manual.*

122

©2009 Sopris West Educational Services. All Rights Reserved.

3. Remind students to check and correct.
   When you finish your assessment, what should you do? (check and correct)
   That's right. Go to the top of the page. Reread the questions and make sure your answers make sense. Fix anything that doesn't sound right. Make sure you have an answer for every question.

4. Remind students what to do when they finish their work.

End of the Unit

In this section, you will find:

Making Decisions

As you near the end of the unit, plan to give the Written Assessment and the Oral Reading Fluency Assessment to each child in your group. Use this section as a general guide for making instructional decisions and doing diagnostic planning.

Written Assessment

The Unit 18 Written Assessment is located on page 119 of *Activity Book 3* and on the CD.

Oral Reading Fluency Assessment

The Unit 18 Oral Reading Fluency Assessment is located on page 127 of this teacher's guide and in the *Assessment Manual.*

Certificate of Achievement

Celebrate your children's accomplishments. When your students master the unit skills, send home the Certificate of Achievement.

Good on ya, mate!

Samantha

has successfully completed

Read Well 2 Unit 18 • The Reef

with 104 words correct per minute.

Teacher Signature Mrs. Smith

Date Feb. 12

Goal Setting

Through goal setting, help your students recognize their accomplishments and learn how to be self-directed learners.

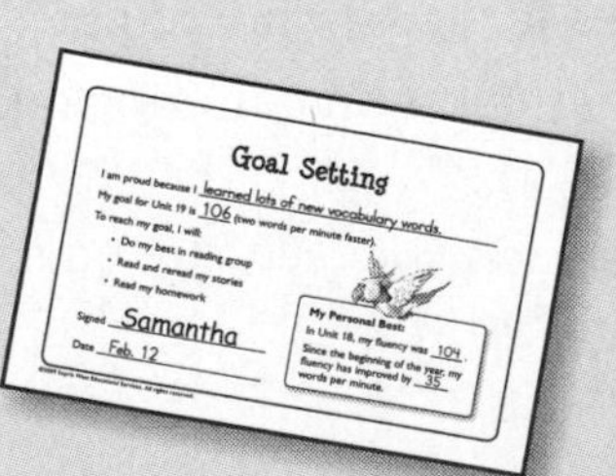

Goal Setting

I am proud because I learned lots of new vocabulary words.

My goal for Unit 19 is 106 (two words per minute faster).

To reach my goal, I will:

- Do my best in reading group
- Read and reread my stories
- Read my homework

Signed Samantha

Date Feb. 12

My Personal Best:

In Unit 18, my fluency was 104.

Since the beginning of the year, my fluency has improved by 35 words per minute.

Extra Practice Lessons

Use the Extra Practice lessons for students who need additional decoding and fluency work. Student materials can be copied from the Extra Practice blackline masters.

Making Decisions

GENERAL ASSESSMENT GUIDELINES

1. After students read Story Reading 6, "Miss Tam Goes Home," give the group the Unit 18 Written Assessment in place of Comprehension and Skill Work. Follow the instructions on pages 120–122 of this guide.

2. While the group is completing the Written Assessment, or any time during the day, administer the Oral Reading Fluency Assessment. Assess each student individually.

   Optional: Graph the results of the assessment. (See Unit 7 Teacher's Guide, pages 92 and 95.)
   - If the student's words correct per minute go up, congratulate the student.
   - If the student's words correct per minute go down, discuss the student's overall improvement and help him or her identify ways to improve for the next assessment.

3. Score oral fluency responses on the Student Assessment Record. Adhere to the scoring criteria in the *Assessment Manual.* Use a stopwatch to time how long it takes each student to read the Oral Reading Fluency Passage, and record errors.

USING WRITTEN ASSESSMENT RESULTS

Results of the Written Assessment *should not* be used to determine whether a student or group of students continues forward in the program. As long as students pass the Oral Reading Fluency Assessment, they should continue forward with the next unit.

The Written Assessment should be used to informally monitor how well students read independently and answer questions in writing. If any student has difficulty with the Written Assessment, re-administer the assessment orally.

If the student has difficulty answering the questions orally:
- Record the types of errors (e.g., main idea, sequencing, open-ended response).
- Provide explicit instruction for these types of questions during reading group, before independent work, and in tutorials, as needed.
  1) Demonstrate (or model) appropriate responses, guide practice, and provide opportunities for independent practice.
  2) For inferential questions, think aloud with students—explain how you arrive at an answer.
  3) For literal questions, teach students to reread a passage, locate information, reread the question, and respond.

USING THE ORAL READING FLUENCY RESULTS

At the end of each unit, you will need to make decisions regarding student progress. Should students go forward in the program? Does the group need Extra Practice before proceeding? Do individuals require more assistance and practice to continue working in their group? These decisions all require use of the oral reading fluency data and professional judgment. As you analyze assessment results, watch for trends and anomalies.

See the *Assessment Manual* for detailed information and instructional recommendations. General guidelines and recommendations follow:

Strong Pass ≥ 120 WCPM 0–2 errors	• Continue with the current pace of instruction. • Have students set goals. (Until students are reading approximately 180 words correct per minute, oral reading fluency continues to be an instructional goal.)
Pass 99–119 WCPM 0–2 errors	• Continue with the current pace of instruction. Consider increasing fluency practice.
No Pass ≤ 98 WCPM	• If a child scores a No Pass but has previously passed all assessments, you may wish to advance the student to the next unit, then carefully monitor the student. • If a child scores a No Pass but has previously passed all assessments, you may wish to advance the student to the next unit and also provide additional practice opportunities. (See below.) • If a child scores two consecutive No Passes or periodic No Passes, additional practice must be provided. (See below.) • If a child scores three consecutive No Passes, the student should be placed in a lower-performing group.

RED FLAG
A No Pass is a red flag. A mild early intervention can prevent an intense and time-consuming intervention in the future.

Added Practice Options for Groups

Warm-Ups:

- Begin each lesson with Partner Reading of the previous day's homework.
- Begin each day with Partner Reading of a Word Fluency from Extra Practice.
- Begin each lesson with a five-minute Fluency Booster. Place copies of the Unit 7–17 *Read Well* Homework in three-ring notebooks. Each day, have students begin Finger Tracking and Whisper Reading at Unit 7, Homework 1. At the end of five minutes, have students mark where they are in their notebooks. The next day, the goal is to read farther.
- Begin each Story Reading with a review of the previous day's story.
- After reading the story, include Short Passage Practice on a daily basis.

Extended Units: If several children begin to score No Passes or barely pass, extend the unit by adding Extra Practices 1, 2, and/or 3. Extra Practice lessons include Decoding Practice, Fluency Passage, Word Fluency, and a Comprehension and Skill Activity. (See pages 130–140 in this guide.)

Jell-Well Reviews: A Jell-Well Review is the *Read Well* term for a review of earlier units. A Jell-Well Review is a period of time taken to celebrate what children have learned and an opportunity to firm up their foundation of learning. To complete a Jell-Well Review, take the group back to the last unit for which all students scored Strong Passes. Then quickly cycle back up. See the *Assessment Manual* for how to build a Jell-Well Review.

Added Practice Options for Individual Students

Tutorials: Set up five-minute tutorials on a daily basis with an assistant, trained volunteer, or cross-age tutor. Have the tutor provide Short Passage Practice and Timed Readings or Extra Practice lessons.

Double Dose: Find ways to provide a double dose of *Read Well* instruction.

- Have the student work in his or her group *and* a lower-performing group.
- Have an instructional assistant, older student, or parent volunteer preview or review lessons.
- Have an instructional assistant provide instruction with Extra Practice lessons.
- Preview new lessons or review previous lessons.

END-OF-THE-UNIT CELEBRATION

When students pass the Oral Reading Fluency Assessment, celebrate with the Certificate of Achievement on page 128.

Note: Using the Flesch-Kincaid Grade Level readability formula, the Unit 18 Assessment has a 2.9 readability level. Readabilities are based on number of words per sentence and number of syllables per word. Adding one or two multisyllabic words can increase readability by a month or two. Though we are attending to readability for the assessments, the overriding factor is decodability.

GOAL SETTING

Goal setting is a powerful tool to help children be active participants in the learning process. You may choose to have students do goal setting on a regular basis or periodically to boost motivation. As students complete their Oral Reading Fluency Assessment, you may wish to say something like:

[Samantha], you read very well! Let's fill out a goal-setting form. It will tell what you are proud of doing in Unit 18 and what you hope to accomplish in Unit 19.

I'm proud of you because you learned so many new vocabulary words. What are some things you are proud of? (I read all my homework . . .)

Let's figure out what to write on your goal-setting form. It says "I am proud because I . . . " What would you like me to write? (I am proud because I learned lots of new vocabulary words.) **Complete the first line of the goal-setting form for the student.**

The next line says, "My goal for Unit 19 is _____." How many words per minute did you read in Unit 18? (104)

Great! We'll write 104 in My Personal Best box. Your goal for Unit 19 is 106. **Fill in the numbers for the student.**

Follow my finger and read the next part of the form. (To reach my goal, I will do my best in reading group, read and reread my stories, read my homework.)

I think you will meet your goal of 106! We'll work together. Maybe you can even beat your goal in Unit 19.

Goal Setting

I am proud because I learned lots of new vocabulary words.

My goal for Unit 19 is 106 (two words per minute faster).

To reach my goal, I will:

- Do my best in reading group
- Read and reread my stories
- Read my homework

Signed Samantha

Date Feb. 12

My Personal Best:
In Unit 18, my fluency was 104.
Since the beginning of the year, my fluency has improved by 35 words per minute.

Help students be in control of their progress by helping them identify what actions they can take to meet their goals. Have students sign the goal-setting form to formalize the goal-setting process.

TRICKY WORD and FOCUS SKILL WARM-UP

chuckled	unusual	library	listened	slither	diving

ORAL READING FLUENCY PASSAGE

Miss Tam's Dream

★After a fun day diving in the sea, Miss Tam was reading	12
a book about the coral reef. She looked at the great pictures and	25
thought about her day. What an adventure! Then Miss Tam's	35
eyes began to close. She was very tired. Soon the book dropped	47
to the floor. Miss Tam was sound asleep.	55
Miss Tam was back at the library reading a story. A giant	67
clam, an orange and white clownfish, and a green sea turtle sat	79
next to her. A huge eel kept sliding off his chair. Then he would	93
slither back onto it. All the animals listened carefully to Miss	104
Tam's story.	106
When Miss Tam finished the story, they all had rice and	117
beans with ice cream. "My, this is unusual," thought Miss Tam.	128
"We're eating snacks in the library."	134
Suddenly Miss Tam opened her eyes. Then she chuckled.	143
"What a dream!" she said.	148

ORAL READING FLUENCY Start timing at the ★. Mark errors. Make a single slash in the text (/) at 60 seconds. If the student completes the passage in less than 60 seconds, have the student go back to the ★ and continue reading. Make a double slash (//) in the text at 60 seconds.

WCPM Determine words correct per minute by subtracting errors from words read in 60 seconds.

STRONG PASS The student scores no more than 2 errors on the first pass through the passage and reads 120 or more words correct per minute. Proceed to Unit 19.

PASS The student scores no more than 2 errors on the first pass through the passage and reads 99 to 119 words correct per minute. Proceed to Unit 19.

NO PASS The student scores 3 or more errors on the first pass through the passage and/or reads 98 or fewer words correct per minute. Provide added fluency practice with *RW2* Unit 18 Extra Practice. (Lessons follow the certificate at the end of the teacher's guide.) After completing the Extra Practice, retest the student.

Good on ya, mate!

____

has successfully completed

Read Well* 2 Unit 18 • *The Reef

with ________ words correct per minute.

Teacher Signature ____________________________

Date ____________________________________

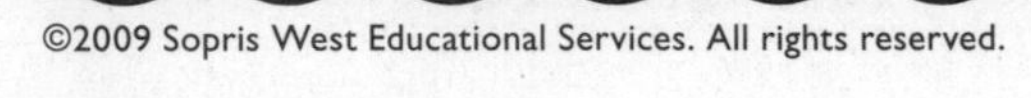

Good on ya, mate!

____

has successfully completed

Read Well* 2 Unit 18 • *The Reef

with ________ words correct per minute.

Teacher Signature ____________________________

Date ____________________________________

Goal Setting

I am proud because I ____

My goal for Unit 19 is _____ (two words per minute faster).

To reach my goal, I will:

- Do my best in reading group
- Read and reread my stories
- Read my homework

My Personal Best:

In Unit 18, my fluency was _____ .

Since the beginning of the year, my fluency has improved by ______ words per minute.

Signed ______________________________

Date ________________________________

Goal Setting

I am proud because I ____

My goal for Unit 19 is _____ (two words per minute faster).

To reach my goal, I will:

- Do my best in reading group
- Read and reread my stories
- Read my homework

My Personal Best:

In Unit 18, my fluency was _____ .

Since the beginning of the year, my fluency has improved by ______ words per minute.

Signed ______________________________

Date ________________________________

PROCEDURES

CAUTION
Your children may not need Extra Practice. Use assessment results to determine if Extra Practice is needed.

1. Sound Review
Use selected Sound Cards from Units 1–18.

2. Sounding Out Smoothly
- For each word, have students say the underlined part, sound out the word smoothly, then read the whole word. Use the words in sentences, as needed.
- Have students read all the words in the row, building accuracy first, then fluency.
- Repeat practice. Mix group and individual turns, independent of your voice.

3. Accuracy and Fluency Building
- For each task, have students say any underlined part, then read each word.
- Set a pace. Then have students read the whole words in each task and column.
- Provide repeated practice, building accuracy first, then fluency.

4. Tricky Words
Have students read each row for accuracy, then fluency.

5. Multisyllabic Words
For each word, have students read each syllable out loud, then tell how many syllables are in the word. If needed, use the word in a sentence. Have students read the whole word.

6. Dictation

peck, pet, Pete, pitch, stitch, switch
- Say "peck." Have students say the word. Have students touch or write the sounds, then read the word. Say something like:

  The first word is ***peck.*** Say the word. (peck)

  What's the first sound? (/p/) Touch under /p/.
  What's the next sound? (/ĕĕĕ/) Write /ĕĕĕ/.
  What's the last sound? (/k/) Touch under /k/.
  Read the word. (peck)

- Repeat with "pet" and "Pete."
- Continue with the rhyming words: pitch, stitch, switch.

EXTRA PRACTICE 1

Unit 18 Decoding Practice

Name ____________________

1. SOUND REVIEW Use selected Sound Cards from Units 1–18.

2. SOUNDING OUT SMOOTHLY Have students say the underlined part, sound out and read each word, then read the row.

scratch	know	wait	blue

3. ACCURACY/FLUENCY BUILDING Have students say any underlined part, then read each word. Next, have students read the column.

A1 Mixed Practice	B1 Bossy E	C1 Rhyming Words	D1 Buildups
over opened return relax tiny itchy story coral little turtle	make making dive diving slide sliding advice tired	picture creature adventure action fiction station **C2** Word Endings cleaner cleaning	fright frighten frightened **D2** Compound Words pufferfish codfish himself Grandfather

4. TRICKY WORDS Have students read each row for accuracy, then fluency.

A	I'll	couldn't	we're	lives	you	5
B	any	against	Mother	friends	said	10

5. MULTISYLLABIC WORDS Have students read the word by parts, tell how many syllables are in the word, then read the whole word.

A	prob•lem	problem	ex•pect	expect
B	re•a•lized	realized	sev•er•al	several
C	an•i•mals	animals	oc•to•pus	octopus

6. DICTATION Say the word. Have students say the word, then say each sound as they touch or write it.

A1 Shifty Words	B1 Rhyming Words
p e ck p e t P e t e	p i t ch s t i t ch s w i t ch

PROCEDURES

1. **First Reading**
   Mix group and individual turns, independent of your voice. Have students work toward an accuracy goal of 0–2 errors and practice any difficult words.

2. **Second Reading, Short Passage Practice: Developing Prosody**
   - Demonstrate how to read a line or two with expression. Read at a rate slightly faster than the students' rate. Say something like:
     Listen as I read the first two sentences with expression and phrasing. I'm going to emphasize certain words and pause between sentences.
     "Pete the Pufferfish had a problem. His skin was itchy."
   - Guide practice with your voice.
     Now read the paragraph with me.
   - Provide individual turns while others track with their fingers and whisper read. Provide descriptive and positive feedback.
     [Anita], you read with wonderful expression!

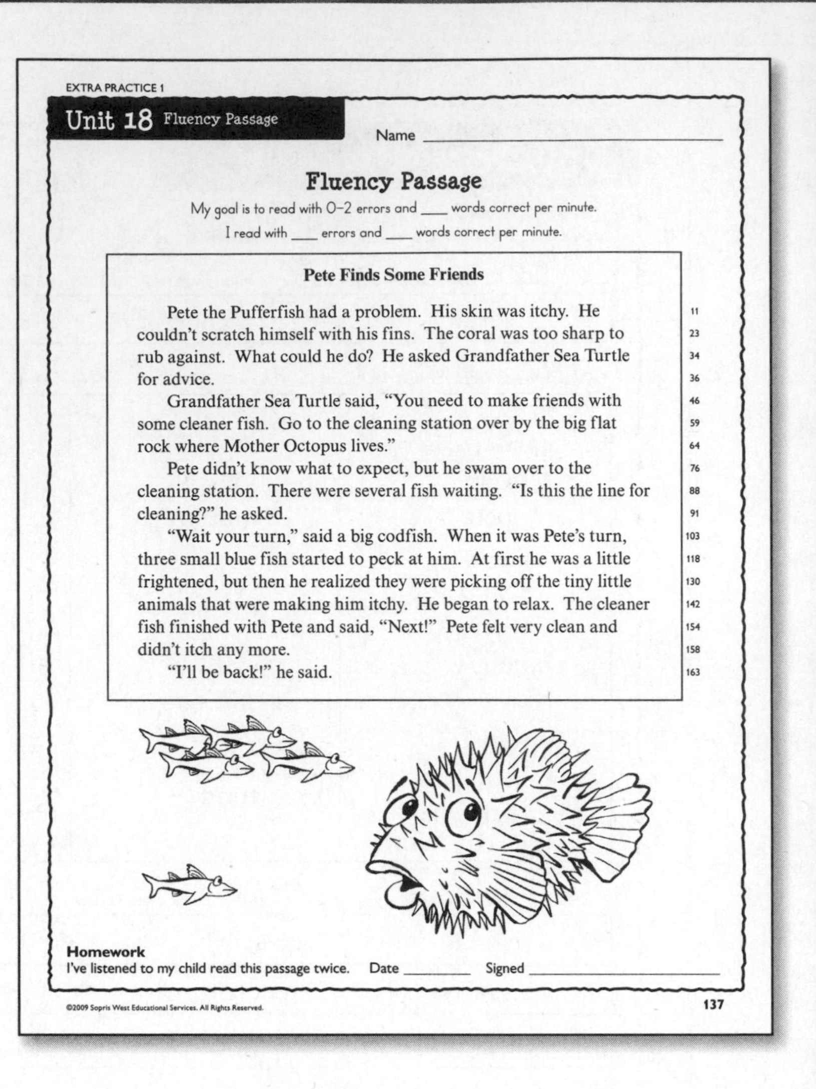

EXTRA PRACTICE 1

Unit 18 Fluency Passage

Name ____________

Fluency Passage

My goal is to read with 0–2 errors and ___ words correct per minute.

I read with ___ errors and ___ words correct per minute.

Pete Finds Some Friends

Pete the Pufferfish had a problem. His skin was itchy. He	11
couldn't scratch himself with his fins. The coral was too sharp to	23
rub against. What could he do? He asked Grandfather Sea Turtle	34
for advice.	36
Grandfather Sea Turtle said, "You need to make friends with	46
some cleaner fish. Go to the cleaning station over by the big flat	59
rock where Mother Octopus lives."	64
Pete didn't know what to expect, but he swam over to the	76
cleaning station. There were several fish waiting. "Is this the line for	88
cleaning?" he asked.	91
"Wait your turn," said a big codfish. When it was Pete's turn,	103
three small blue fish started to peck at him. At first he was a little	118
frightened, but then he realized they were picking off the tiny little	130
animals that were making him itchy. He began to relax. The cleaner	142
fish finished with Pete and said, "Next!" Pete felt very clean and	154
didn't itch any more.	158
"I'll be back!" he said.	163

Homework
I've listened to my child read this passage twice. Date ______ Signed ____________

©2009 Sopris West Educational Services. All Rights Reserved.

137

3. **Partner Reading: Repeated Reading (Checkout Opportunity)**

While students do Partner Reading, listen to individuals read the passage. Work on accuracy and fluency, as needed.

4. **Homework: Repeated Reading**

Have students read the story at home.

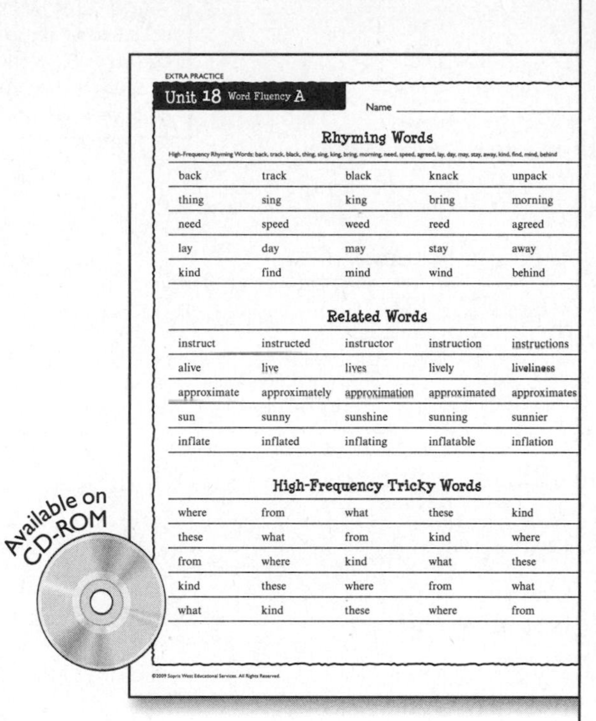

EXTRA PRACTICE

Unit 18 Word Fluency A

Name ____________

Rhyming Words

High-Frequency Rhyming Words: back, track, black, thing, sing, king, bring, morning, need, speed, agreed, lay, day, may, stay, away, kind, find, mind, behind

back	track	black	knack	unpack
thing	sing	king	bring	morning
need	speed	weed	reed	agreed
lay	day	may	stay	away
kind	find	mind	wind	behind

Related Words

instruct	instructed	instructor	instruction	instructions
alive	live	lives	lively	liveliness
approximate	approximately	approximation	approximated	approximates
sun	sunny	sunshine	sunning	sunnier
inflate	inflated	inflating	inflatable	inflation

High-Frequency Tricky Words

where	from	what	these	kind
these	what	from	kind	where
from	where	kind	what	these
kind	these	where	from	what
what	kind	these	where	from

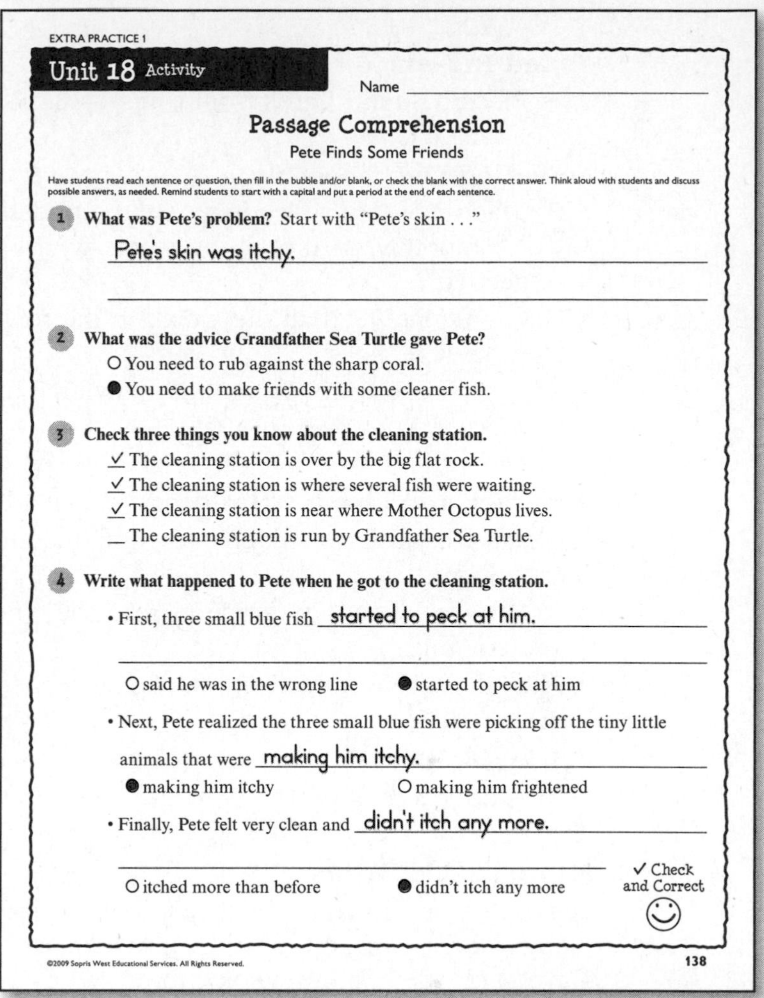

EXTRA PRACTICE 1

Unit 18 Activity

Name ____________

Passage Comprehension

Pete Finds Some Friends

Have students read each sentence or question, then fill in the bubble and/or blank, or check the blank with the correct answer. Think aloud with students and discuss possible answers, as needed. Remind students to start with a capital and put a period at the end of each sentence.

1. **What was Pete's problem?** Start with "Pete's skin . . ."
   Pete's skin was itchy.

2. **What was the advice Grandfather Sea Turtle gave Pete?**
   ○ You need to rub against the sharp coral.
   ● You need to make friends with some cleaner fish.

3. **Check three things you know about the cleaning station.**
   ✓ The cleaning station is over by the big flat rock.
   ✓ The cleaning station is where several fish were waiting.
   ✓ The cleaning station is near where Mother Octopus lives.
   __ The cleaning station is run by Grandfather Sea Turtle.

4. **Write what happened to Pete when he got to the cleaning station.**
   • First, three small blue fish started to peck at him.
   ○ said he was in the wrong line ● started to peck at him
   • Next, Pete realized the three small blue fish were picking off the tiny little animals that were making him itchy.
   ● making him itchy ○ making him frightened
   • Finally, Pete felt very clean and didn't itch any more.
   ○ itched more than before ● didn't itch any more

✓ Check and Correct

138

PROCEDURES

For each step, demonstrate and guide practice, as needed. Then have students complete the page independently.

ACCURACY BEFORE FLUENCY (Reminder)

Word Fluency is designed to build accuracy and fluency. Students should practice for accuracy before working on fluency.

1. Activity
Passage Comprehension

- Have students read each sentence or question, then fill in the bubble and/or blank or check the blank with the correct answer.
- Think aloud with students and discuss the multiple-choice options, as needed.

Self-monitoring

Have students read and check their work, then draw a happy face in the Check and Correct circle.

2. Word Fluency (BLMs are located on the CD.)

- To build fluency, have students read Rhyming Words, Related Words, and High-Frequency Tricky Words. Have students read each section three times in a row.
- To build accuracy, have students read all sets with partners.

PROCEDURES

CAUTION
Your children may not need Extra Practice. Use assessment results to determine if Extra Practice is needed.

1. Sound Review

Use selected Sound Cards from Units 1–18.

2. Sounding Out Smoothly

- For each word, have students say the underlined part, sound out the word smoothly, then read the whole word. Use the words in sentences, as needed.
- Have students read all the words in the row, building accuracy first, then fluency.
- Repeat practice. Mix group and individual turns, independent of your voice.

3. Accuracy and Fluency Building

- For each task, have students say any underlined part, then read each word.
- Set a pace. Then have students read the whole words in each task and column.
- Provide repeated practice, building accuracy first, then fluency.

4. Tricky Words

Have students read each row for accuracy, then fluency.

5. Multisyllabic Words

For each word, have students read each syllable out loud, then tell how many syllables are in the word. If needed, use the word in a sentence. Have students read the whole word.

6. Dictation

reach, rear, near, dream, cream, scream

- Say "reach." Have students say the word. Have students touch or write the sounds, then read the word.

  The first word is ***reach.*** Say the word. (reach)

  What's the first sound? (/rrr/) Touch under /rrr/.
  What's the next sound? (/ēēē/) Write /ēēē/ with the e-a pattern.
  What's the last sound? (/ch/) Touch under /ch/.
  Read the word. (reach)

- Repeat with "rear" and "near."
- Continue with the rhyming words: dream, cream, scream.

EXTRA PRACTICE 2

Unit 18 Decoding Practice

Name ______________________

1. SOUND REVIEW Use selected Sound Cards from Units 1–18.

2. SOUNDING OUT SMOOTHLY Have students say the underlined part, sound out and read each word, then read the row.

shores	reefs	food	first

3. ACCURACY/FLUENCY BUILDING Have students say any underlined part, then read each word. Next, have students read the column.

A1 Mixed Practice	B1 Word Endings	C1 Rhyming Words	D1 Compound Words
also	drop	rice	seahorses
coral	dropped	price	pufferfish
giant		twice	clownfish
after	visitors	**C2 Bossy E**	fishermen
slither	octopuses	waves	**D2 Multisyllabic Words**
reasons	showing	homes	finally
depend	reading	close	carefully
provide	chuckled	huge	suddenly
protect	finished		dangerous

4. TRICKY WORDS Have students read each row for accuracy, then fluency.

A	living	become	who	are	what	5
B	islands	ocean	learned	learning	thought	10

5. MULTISYLLABIC WORDS Have students read the word by parts, tell how many syllables are in the word, then read the whole word.

A	im•por•tant	important	sci•en•tists	scientists
B	li•brar•y	library	con•ti•nents	continents
C	med•i•cines	medicines	un•u•su•al	unusual

6. DICTATION Say the word. Have students say the word, then say each sound as they touch or write it.

A1 Shifty Words	B1 Rhyming Words
r e a ch	d r e a m
r ea r	c r e a m
n ea r	s c r e a m

PROCEDURES

1. First Reading

Mix group and individual turns, independent of your voice. Have students work toward an accuracy goal of 0–2 errors and practice any difficult words.

2. Second Reading, Timed Reading: Repeated Reading

- Once the group accuracy goal has been achieved, time individual students for 30 or 60 seconds while the other children track with their fingers and whisper read.
- Determine words correct per minute. Record student scores. Celebrate when students reach their goals!

Wow! [Rashad], you met your goal. That was your best score ever. You get to read to the principal this week.

3. Partner Reading: Repeated Reading (Checkout Opportunity)

While students do Partner Reading, listen to individuals read the passage. Work on accuracy and fluency, as needed.

4. Homework: Repeated Reading

Have students read the story at home.

EXTRA PRACTICE 2

Unit 18 Fluency Passage

Name ______________________

Fluency Passage

My goal is to read with 0–2 errors and ___ words correct per minute.

I read with ___ errors and ___ words correct per minute.

Coral Reefs Are Important

Coral reefs are important for many reasons. First, many fish 10
and other animals depend on coral reefs. Seahorses, octopuses, 19
pufferfish, and other fish and animals make their homes on the reefs. 31

People also depend on coral reefs. The reefs provide jobs. 41
People who live near the reef can make a living showing visitors the 54
reef, or they can become fishermen. Reef fish and other animals are 66
food for people. 69

Next, coral reefs are important because they protect islands from 79
big waves. Reefs protect the shores of continents from big waves too. 91
Big ocean waves hit the reef first and slow down. Then when the 104
waves reach the shore, they are not so dangerous. 113

Finally, scientists have learned that coral reef animals are 122
important. Scientists are learning how to use many of the coral reef 134
animals to make new medicines. 139

Homework
I've listened to my child read this passage twice. Date ________ Signed ______________________

©2009 Sopris West Educational Services. All Rights Reserved.

140

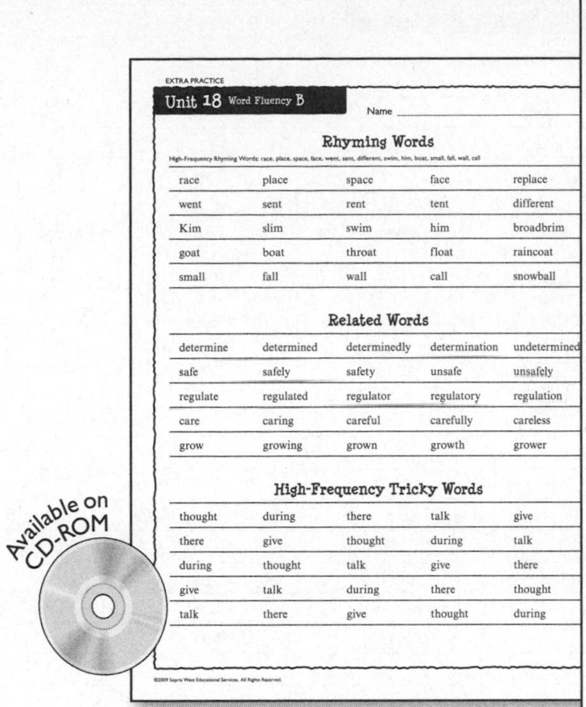

EXTRA PRACTICE

Unit 18 Word Fluency B

Name ______

Rhyming Words

High-Frequency Rhyming Words: race, place, space, face, went, sent, different, swim, him, boat, small, fall, wall, call

race	place	space	face	replace
went	sent	rent	tent	different
Kim	slim	swim	him	broadbrim
goat	boat	throat	float	raincoat
small	fall	wall	call	snowball

Related Words

determine	determined	determinedly	determination	undetermined
safe	safely	safety	unsafe	unsafely
regulate	regulated	regulator	regulatory	regulation
care	caring	careful	carefully	careless
grow	growing	grown	growth	grower

High-Frequency Tricky Words

thought	during	there	talk	give
there	give	thought	during	talk
during	thought	talk	give	there
give	talk	during	there	thought
talk	there	give	thought	during

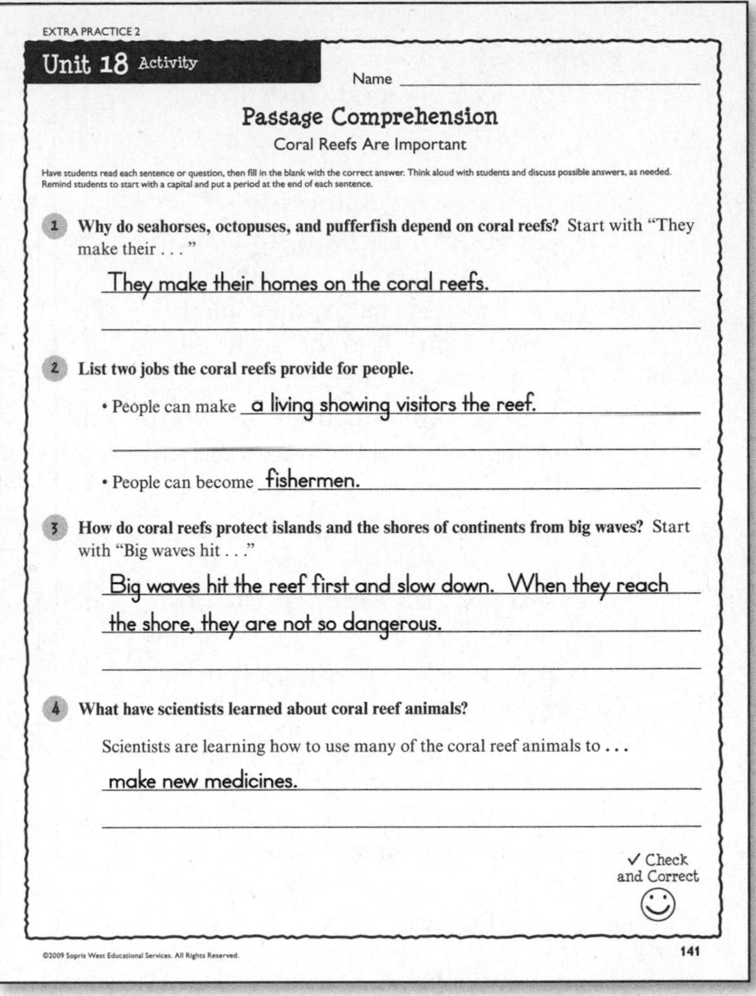

EXTRA PRACTICE 2

Unit 18 Activity

Name ______

Passage Comprehension

Coral Reefs Are Important

Have students read each sentence or question, then fill in the blank with the correct answer. Think aloud with students and discuss possible answers, as needed. Remind students to start with a capital and put a period at the end of each sentence.

1. **Why do seahorses, octopuses, and pufferfish depend on coral reefs?** Start with "They make their . . ."

   They make their homes on the coral reefs.

2. **List two jobs the coral reefs provide for people.**

   - People can make a living showing visitors the reef.
   - People can become fishermen.

3. **How do coral reefs protect islands and the shores of continents from big waves?** Start with "Big waves hit . . ."

   Big waves hit the reef first and slow down. When they reach the shore, they are not so dangerous.

4. **What have scientists learned about coral reef animals?**

   Scientists are learning how to use many of the coral reef animals to . . .

   make new medicines.

✓ Check and Correct

141

PROCEDURES

For each step, demonstrate and guide practice, as needed. Then have students complete the page independently.

1. Activity
Passage Comprehension

Have students read each sentence or question, then fill in the blank with the correct answer.

Self-monitoring

Have students read and check their work, then draw a happy face in the Check and Correct circle.

2. Word Fluency (BLMs are located on the CD.)

- To build fluency, have students read Rhyming Words, Related Words, and High-Frequency Tricky Words. Have students read each section three times in a row.
- To build accuracy, have students read all sets with partners.

ACCURACY BEFORE FLUENCY (Reminder)

Word Fluency is designed to build accuracy and fluency. Students should practice for accuracy before working on fluency.

PROCEDURES

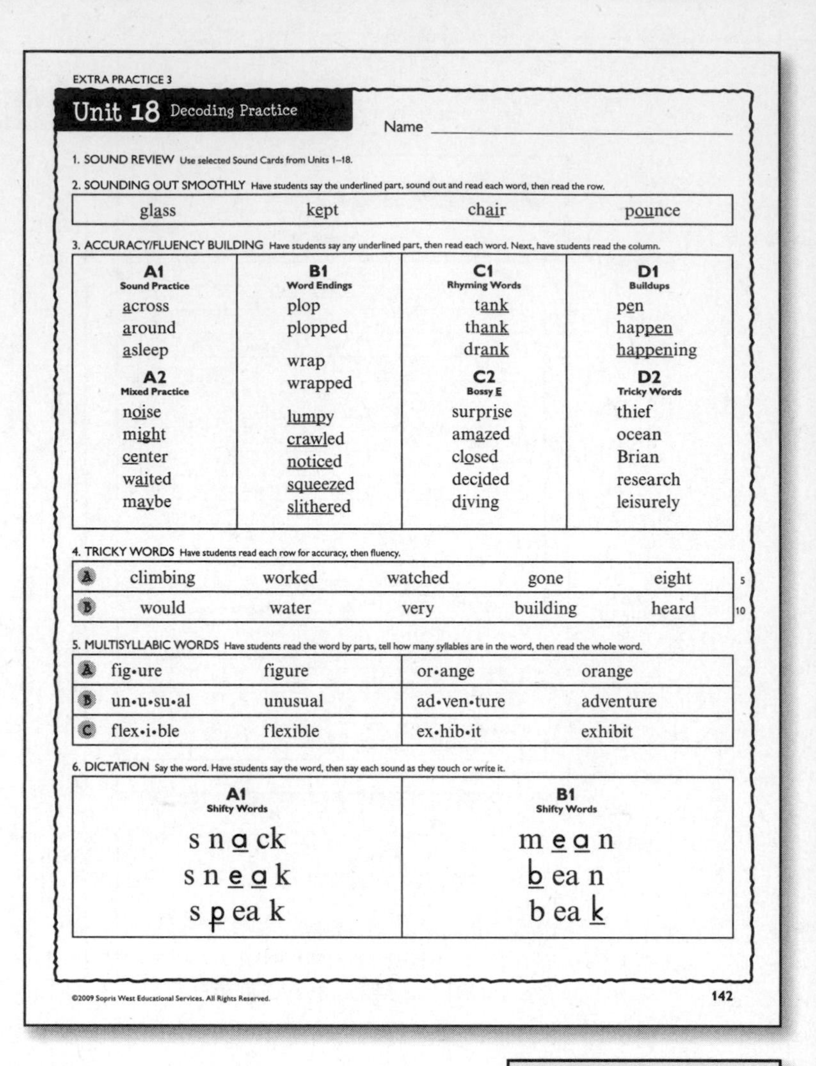

EXTRA PRACTICE 3

Unit 18 Decoding Practice

Name ____________________

1. SOUND REVIEW Use selected Sound Cards from Units 1–18.

2. SOUNDING OUT SMOOTHLY Have students say the underlined part, sound out and read each word, then read the row.

glass	kept	chair	pounce

3. ACCURACY/FLUENCY BUILDING Have students say any underlined part, then read each word. Next, have students read the column.

A1 Sound Practice	B1 Word Endings	C1 Rhyming Words	D1 Buildups
across	plop	tank	pen
around	plopped	thank	happen
asleep	wrap	drank	happening
	wrapped		
A2 Mixed Practice		**C2 Bossy E**	**D2 Tricky Words**
noise	lumpy	surprise	thief
might	crawled	amazed	ocean
center	noticed	closed	Brian
waited	squeezed	decided	research
maybe	slithered	diving	leisurely

4. TRICKY WORDS Have students read each row for accuracy, then fluency.

A	climbing	worked	watched	gone	eight	5
B	would	water	very	building	heard	10

5. MULTISYLLABIC WORDS Have students read the word by parts, tell how many syllables are in the word, then read the whole word.

A	fig•ure	figure	or•ange	orange
B	un•u•su•al	unusual	ad•ven•ture	adventure
C	flex•i•ble	flexible	ex•hib•it	exhibit

6. DICTATION Say the word. Have students say the word, then say each sound as they touch or write it.

A1 Shifty Words	B1 Shifty Words
s n a ck	m e a n
s n e a k	b ea n
s p ea k	b ea k

142

1. Sound Review

Use selected Sound Cards from Units 1–18.

2. Sounding Out Smoothly

- For each word, have students say the underlined part, sound out the word smoothly, then read the whole word. Use the words in sentences, as needed.
- Have students read all the words in the row, building accuracy first, then fluency.
- Repeat practice.

3. Accuracy and Fluency Building

- For each task, have students say any underlined part, then read each word.
- Set a pace. Then have students read the whole words in each task and column.
- Provide repeated practice, building accuracy first, then fluency.

4. Tricky Words

Have students read each row for accuracy, then fluency.

CAUTION

Your children may not need Extra Practice. Use assessment results to determine if Extra Practice is needed.

5. Multisyllabic Words

For each word, have students read each syllable out loud, then tell how many syllables are in the word. If needed, use the word in a sentence. Have students read the whole word.

6. Dictation

snack, sneak, speak, mean, bean, beak

- Say "snack." Have students say the word. Have students touch or write the sounds, then read the word. Say something like:

  The first word is ***snack.*** Say the word. (snack)

  What's the first sound? (/sss/) Touch under /sss/.
  What's the next sound? (/nnn/) Touch under /nnn/.
  What's the first sound? (/ăăă/) Write /ăăă/.
  What's the last sound? (/k/) Touch under /k/.
  Read the word. (snack)

- Repeat with "sneak" and "speak."
- Continue with the shifty words: mean, bean, beak.

PROCEDURES

1. First Reading

Mix group and individual turns, independent of your voice. Have students work toward an accuracy goal of 0–2 errors and practice any difficult words.

2. Second Reading, Short Passage Practice: Developing Prosody

- Demonstrate how to read a line or two with expression. Read at a rate slightly faster than the students' rate. Say something like:
  Listen as I read the first two sentences with expression and phrasing. I'm going to emphasize certain words and pause between sentences.
  "Brian worked at the Center for Ocean Research. One morning, he noticed that some crabs were missing from a tank near the octopus exhibit."
- Guide practice with your voice.
  Now read the paragraph with me.
- Provide individual turns while others track with their fingers and whisper read. Provide descriptive and positive feedback.
  [Micah], you read with wonderful expression!

EXTRA PRACTICE 3

Unit 18 Fluency Passage

Name ______________________

Fluency Passage

My goal is to read with 0–2 errors and ___ words correct per minute.

I read with ___ errors and ___ words correct per minute.

The Sneak Thief

Brian worked at the Center for Ocean Research. One morning, he noticed that some crabs were missing from a tank near the octopus exhibit. No one could figure out where they might have gone. The next morning, more crabs were missing. Brian decided to stay in the building that night. Maybe he would see what was happening to the crabs. (10, 22, 33, 43, 56, 60)

The Center closed for the night. Brian watched and waited by the crab exhibit. Then he heard a noise by the octopus tank. To his surprise, Lumpy the octopus was squeezing out of a little hole! She slithered across the floor to the crab tank, crawled up the glass side, and plopped into the water. Brian watched as she pounced on a crab, wrapped her eight flexible arms around it, and bit it with her sharp beak. Lumpy had a leisurely meal, and then crawled back over to her own tank. Brian was amazed. Lumpy was the sneak thief! (71, 85, 97, 110, 122, 135, 146, 158, 159)

Homework

I've listened to my child read this passage twice. Date ________ Signed ________________

143

3. Partner Reading: Repeated Reading (Checkout Opportunity)

While students do Partner Reading, listen to individuals read the passage. Work on accuracy and fluency, as needed.

4. Homework: Repeated Reading

Have students read the story at home.

PROCEDURES

For each step, demonstrate and guide practice, as needed. Then have students complete the page independently.

1. Activity
Passage Comprehension

- Have students read each sentence or question, then fill in the bubble and/or blank with the correct answer.
- Think aloud with students and discuss the multiple-choice options, as needed.

Self-monitoring

Have students read and check their work, then draw a happy face in the Check and Correct circle.

2. Word Fluency (BLMs are located on the CD.)

You may wish to have students repeat practice with Extra Practice, Word Fluency A or B.

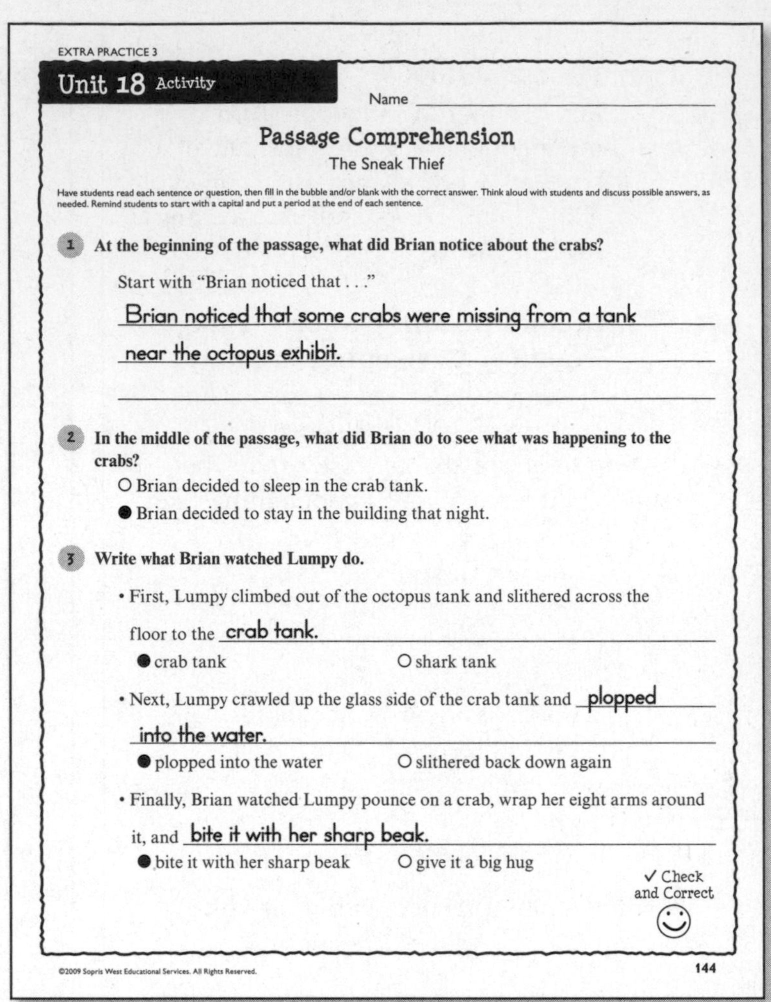
EXTRA PRACTICE 3

Unit 18 Activity

Name

Passage Comprehension

The Sneak Thief

Have students read each sentence or question, then fill in the bubble and/or blank with the correct answer. Think aloud with students and discuss possible answers, as needed. Remind students to start with a capital and put a period at the end of each sentence.

1. **At the beginning of the passage, what did Brian notice about the crabs?**

Start with "Brian noticed that . . ."

Brian noticed that some crabs were missing from a tank near the octopus exhibit.

2. **In the middle of the passage, what did Brian do to see what was happening to the crabs?**

○ Brian decided to sleep in the crab tank.
● Brian decided to stay in the building that night.

3. **Write what Brian watched Lumpy do.**

- First, Lumpy climbed out of the octopus tank and slithered across the floor to the crab tank.
  ● crab tank ○ shark tank
- Next, Lumpy crawled up the glass side of the crab tank and plopped into the water.
  ● plopped into the water ○ slithered back down again
- Finally, Brian watched Lumpy pounce on a crab, wrap her eight arms around it, and bite it with her sharp beak.
  ● bite it with her sharp beak ○ give it a big hug

✓ Check and Correct

144